PRAYING GOD'S WILL

for My Husband

LEE ROBERTS

OLIVER
NELSON

THOMAS NELSON PUBLISHERS
Nashville

To
my mom,
Genevieve Roberts,
and to
the loving memory of my dad,
J. T. Roberts

Copyright © 1993 by Lee Roberts

All rights reserved. Written permission must be secured from the publisher to use or reproduce any part of this book, except for brief quotations in critical reviews or articles.

Published in Nashville, Tennessee, by Oliver-Nelson Books, a division of Thomas Nelson, Inc., Publishers

The Bible version used in this publication is THE NEW KING JAMES VERSION. Copyright © 1979, 1980, 1982, Thomas Nelson, Inc., Publishers. Verses have been modified to fit the prayer format.

Printed in the United States of America.

Library of Congress Cataloging-in-Publication Data

Roberts, Lee, 1941-
    Praying God's will for my husband / Lee Roberts.
      p.   cm.
    ISBN 0-8407-9176-3 (pbk.)
    1. Wives—Prayer-books and devotions—English. 2. Husbands-
-Religious life. 3. Christian life—1960- I. Title.
BV283.W6R575 1993
242'.843—dc20   92-35466
                                     CIP

9 10 11 12 13 — 97 96

Contents

For Women Only

As a Christian wife, you have no greater privilege nor any higher calling than to constantly, and on a day-by-day basis, lift up your husband by name in prayer. If you understand it or not, you have a tremendous responsibility before God on his behalf. That responsibility is so great that unless he has your constant prayer support, he cannot become all that he should be. Nor can he become the husband and spiritual leader of the home that he should be. He is responsible before God for your spiritual, emotional, and physical well-being. He is to give you his loving, prayerful support in every area of your life.

The question now becomes, "What do I pray?" As a Christian, your role model for prayer must be Jesus. In Matthew 4:4, Jesus tells us that, "Man shall not live by bread alone, but by every word that proceeds from the mouth of God." In Ephesians 6:17, God tells us that the sword of the Spirit "is the word of God."

What should you pray for your husband? Scripture is clear that you should pray God's word for him. At the same time you must never forget that God is a sovereign God and that He is not obligated to a name-it-and-claim-it theology. God will always do what is best for you and your husband. But at the same time you will do well to understand that when you pray God's word for your husband, you are actually praying both the mind and the perfect will of God for him.

There is no better way to pray for your husband than to pray God's mind and will for him. Follow a systematic plan of praying God's will for your husband and you will see dynamic growth take place in his life as he becomes the husband God intended for you.

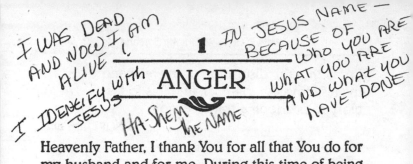

ANGER

Handwritten annotations:
I WAS DEAD AND NOW I AM ALIVE !
I IDENTIFY with JESUS
IN JESUS NAME — BECAUSE OF Who you ARE
WHAT you ARE AND WHAT you hAVE DONE
HA-ShEM ThE NAME

Heavenly Father, I thank You for all that You do for my husband and for me. During this time of being alone with You I ask You, in Jesus' name, to hear Your word as my prayers concerning any anger that may abide in my husband. Your word is clear that anger does not produce the righteousness that You want in each of us. I petition You now, with Your very words, to remove any anger from my husband that may be a stumbling block in his walk with You. Thank You, God, for answering these my prayers for my husband. Amen.

God, in accordance with Your Word...

I pray that my husband will be swift to hear, slow to speak, slow to wrath; for his wrath does not produce the righteousness of God.

JAMES 1:19–20

I pray that the discretion of my husband makes him slow to anger, and it is to his glory to overlook a transgression.

PROVERBS 19:11

———— ◆ ————

I pray that my husband will commit his way to You, LORD, and trust also in You, and You shall bring it to pass. You shall bring forth his righteousness as the light, and his justice as the noonday. I pray that he will rest in you, LORD, and wait patiently for you. I pray that he does not fret because of him who prospers in his way or because of the person who brings wicked schemes to pass. I pray that he will cease from anger, and forsake wrath; that he does not fret—it only causes harm.

PSALM 37:5–8

———— ◆ ————

I pray that my husband will not hasten in his spirit to be angry, for anger rests in the bosom of fools.

ECCLESIASTES 7:9

2

I pray that my husband will let all bitterness, wrath, anger, clamor, and evil speaking be put away from him, with all malice. I pray also that he will be kind to others, tenderhearted, forgiving others, just as God in Christ also forgave him.

EPHESIANS 4:31–32

I pray that my husband understands that a fool vents all his feelings, but a wise person holds his back.

PROVERBS 29:11

I pray that my husband knows that being slow to anger is better than the mighty, and ruling his spirit is better than taking a city.

PROVERBS 16:32

I pray that my husband realizes that a person who is quick-tempered acts foolishly.

PROVERBS 14:17

I pray that if my husband is angry, he will not sin. That he does not let the sun go down on his wrath.

EPHESIANS 4:26

I pray that my husband will make no friendship with an angry person and with a furious man he does not go lest he learn their ways and sets a snare for his soul.

PROVERBS 22:24–25

I pray that my husband always remembers that a soft answer turns away wrath, but a harsh word stirs up anger.

PROVERBS 15:1

2

ATTITUDE

Lord Jesus, I ask You now, using the very words that have been given to me in the Holy Scripture, to make certain that my husband always has an attitude of joy in You and an attitude and an expectancy that he can do all things through You who give him Your strength to face the issues and problems of life. Thank You, LORD, for his happiness and his joy. In Your name I pray. Amen.

God, in accordance
with Your Word...

I pray that my husband knows that he can do all things through Christ who strengthens him.

PHILIPPIANS 4:13

I pray that my husband will not sorrow, for the joy of the LORD is his strength.

NEHEMIAH 8:10

I pray that my husband will remember
whatever things are true, whatever
things are noble, whatever things are just,
whatever things are pure, whatever
things are lovely, whatever things are of
good report, if there is any virtue and
if there is anything praiseworthy—that he
will meditate on these things.

PHILIPPIANS 4:8

I pray that my husband will remember that
this is the day which the LORD has made
and that he will rejoice and be glad in it.

PSALM 118:24

I pray that my husband understands what
Jesus meant when He said, "My grace
is sufficient for you, for My strength is made
perfect in weakness."

2 CORINTHIANS 12:9

I pray that my husband realizes that in all
these things he is more than a
conqueror through You who loved him.

ROMANS 8:37

---◆---

I pray that my husband will always love
You, the Lord his God, with all his heart,
with all his soul, with all his mind, and
with all his strength and that he will
love his neighbor as himself.

MARK 12:30–31

---◆---

I pray that whatever my husband does he
does it heartily, as to You, Lord, and
not to men.

COLOSSIANS 3:23

3

CONDEMNED

Lord God, I come before You at this moment to ask You to keep in my husband's mind at all times the knowledge that there is no condemnation for those that are in Christ Jesus. Help him to know that if he trusts in Jesus he need not let Satan bring thoughts of doubt and condemnation. Thank You, Lord, for removing all such thoughts and feelings from my husband. Thank You in Jesus' name. Amen.

**God, in accordance
with Your Word...**

I pray that my husband will draw near with
a true heart in full assurance of faith,
having his heart sprinkled from an evil
conscience and his body washed with
pure water.

HEBREWS 10:22

I pray that my husband always remembers that You, the LORD his God, are gracious and merciful, and will not turn Your face from him if he returns to You.

2 CHRONICLES 30:9

I pray that my husband knows that it was You, God, who said that, "I, even I, am He who blots out your transgressions for My own sake."

ISAIAH 43:25

I pray, God, that You did not send Your Son into the world to condemn my husband, but that my husband through Him might be saved. He who believes in Him is not condemned.

JOHN 3:17–18

I pray that my husband, who hears Your word and believes in Him who sent You has everlasting life, and shall not come into judgment, but has passed from death into life.

JOHN 5:24

I pray that You, God, will be merciful to
my husband's unrighteousness, and to
his sins and to his lawless deeds and that
You remember them no more.

HEBREWS 8:12

I pray that my husband will forsake any
wicked ways and any unrighteous
thoughts. Let him return to You, LORD , and
You will have mercy on him and
abundantly pardon him.

ISAIAH/55:7

I pray that my husband will acknowledge
his sin to You, God, and his iniquity he
has not hidden. That he will confess
his transgressions to You so You can
forgive the iniquity of his sins.

PSALM 32:5

I pray that if my husband will confess his
sins, You, God, are faithful and just to
forgive his sins and to cleanse him from
all unrighteousness.

1 JOHN 1:9

◆

I pray that there is therefore now no
condemnation to my husband who is
in Christ Jesus, who does not walk according
to the flesh, but according to the Spirit.
For the law of the Spirit of life in Christ
Jesus has made him free from the law
of sin and death.

ROMANS 8:1–2

◆

I pray that as far as the east is from the
west, so far have You removed my
husband's transgressions from him.

PSALM 103:12

I pray that if my husband is in You, Christ, he is a new creation; old things have passed away; behold, all things have become new.

2 CORINTHIANS 5:17

———————◆———————

I pray that my husband is blessed, whose transgression is forgiven, whose sin is covered.

PSALM 32:1

———————◆———————

I pray that my husband has overcome Satan by the blood of the Lamb and by the word of his testimony.

REVELATION 12:11

———————◆———————

I pray that my husband remembers that Jesus Himself said, "Neither do I condemn you; go and sin no more."

JOHN 8:11

I pray, God, that You will forgive my
husband's iniquity, and his sin and will
remember them no more.

JEREMIAH 31:34

4
CONFIDENCE

Lord Jesus, based upon God's word I call upon You to literally fill my husband with confidence. Give him the spiritual confidence to know that whatever he asks in Your name he will receive. Fill him with the confidence that only You can give. Thank You for honoring Your word and my prayers. Amen.

God, in accordance with Your Word...

I pray that when my husband passes through the waters, You will be with him; and through the rivers, they shall not overflow him. When he walks through the fire, he shall not be burned, nor shall the flame scorch him.

ISAIAH 43:2

———————◆———————

I pray, God, that my husband always remembers that it is You who justifies.

ROMANS 8:33

I pray that this is the confidence that my husband has in You, Jesus, that if he asks anything according to Your will, You hear him. And if he knows that You hear him, whatever he asks, he knows that he has the petitions that he asked of You.

1 JOHN 5:14–15

I pray that when my husband faces an obstacle he always remembers that God has said that it is "Not by might nor by power, but by My Spirit."

ZECHARIAH 4:6

I pray that whatever my husband asks in Jesus' name, You will do it.

JOHN 14:14

I pray that You, the LORD God, are my husband's strength.

HABAKKUK 3:19

I pray that my husband will not cast away
his confidence, which has great reward.
For he has need of endurance, so that
after he has done the will of You, God,
he may receive the promise.

HEBREWS 10:35–36

I pray that my husband will be confident
of this very thing, that You who have
begun a good work in him will complete it
until the day of Jesus Christ.

PHILIPPIANS 1:6

I pray that my husband can do all things
through Christ who strengthens him.

PHILIPPIANS 4:13

I pray that my husband may boldly say:
"The Lord is my helper; I will not fear.
What can man do to me?"

HEBREWS 13:6

I pray that if my husband's heart does not condemn him, he will have confidence toward You, God.

1 JOHN 3:21

---◆---

I pray that if my husband will wait on You, LORD, he shall renew his strength. He shall mount up with wings like eagles, he shall run and not be weary, he shall walk and not faint.

ISAIAH 40:31

5

CONFUSED

Heavenly Father, in the beautiful and precious name of Jesus, my Lord and Savior, I ask You to remove all confusion from my husband. Help him to know that Your word says You are the author of peace and not of confusion and that he is to lean on You and Your word and not his own understanding. Thank You in Jesus' name for honoring this my prayer for my wonderful and precious husband. Amen.

**God, in accordance
with Your Word...**

I pray that my husband will trust in You, LORD, with all his heart, and lean not on his own understanding. I pray that in all his ways he will acknowledge You, and You will direct his paths.

PROVERBS 3:5–6

I pray that You, God, will instruct my husband and teach him in the way he should go.

PSALM 32:8

I pray that my husband has great peace because he loves Your law, and nothing can cause him to stumble.

PSALM 119:165

I pray that my husband will always cast his burdens on You, LORD, and You shall sustain him.

PSALM 55:22

I pray that my husband will always remember that God gives power to the weak, and to those who have no might He increases strength.

ISAIAH 40:29

I pray that when my husband passes
through the waters, You will be with
him. And when he passes through the
rivers, they shall not overflow him.
When he walks through the fire, he shall
not be burned, nor shall the flame
scorch him. For You are the LORD his God.

ISAIAH 43:2

I pray that my husband will be anxious for
nothing, but in everything by prayer
and supplication, with thanksgiving, let his
requests be made known to You, God,
and the peace of God, which surpasses all
understanding, will guard his heart and
mind through Christ Jesus.

PHILIPPIANS 4:6–7

I pray that when my husband feels
confused he will remember and
understand that You, God, are not the
author of confusion but of peace.

1 CORINTHIANS 14:33

I pray, God, that You have not given my
husband a spirit of fear, but of power
and of love and of a sound mind.

2 TIMOTHY 1:7

◆

I pray that my husband will not think it
strange concerning the fiery trial which
is to try him, as though some strange thing
happened to him; but that he will rejoice
to the extent that he partakes of Christ's
sufferings, that when His glory is
revealed, he also may be glad with
exceeding joy.

1 PETER 4:12–13

◆

I pray that if my husband lacks wisdom, let
him ask of You, God, who gives to all
liberally and without reproach, and it will
be given to him.

JAMES 1:5

I pray that my husband knows that where
envy and self-seeking exist, confusion
and every evil thing will be there. But the
wisdom that is from above is first pure,
then peaceable, gentle, willing to yield, full
of mercy and good fruits, without
partiality and without hypocrisy.

JAMES 3:16–17

I pray that You, LORD God, will help my
husband; therefore he will not be
disgraced.

ISAIAH 50:7

6

COURAGE

Perfect God, grant my husband the courage that only You can give. Help him to remember that You promised in Your word that he can do all things through Jesus and that he should never be afraid or discouraged or dismayed because You, his God, will be with him always. Thank You, God, in Jesus' name, for filling my husband with courage. Amen.

**God, in accordance
with Your Word...**

I pray that my husband will be persuaded
that neither death nor life, nor angels
nor principalities nor powers, nor things
present nor things to come, nor height
nor depth, nor any other created thing,
shall be able to separate him from the
love of God which is in Christ Jesus his
Lord.

ROMANS 8:38–39

I pray that my husband will always fear
not, for You God are with him. I pray
that he will not be dismayed, for You are
his God. I pray that You will strengthen
him and help him and that You will uphold
him with Your righteous right hand.

ISAIAH 41:10

I pray that my husband shall not die, but
live, and declare the works of the LORD.

PSALM 118:17

I pray that You, the eternal God, are my
husband's refuge and that You will thrust
out the enemy from before him.

DEUTERONOMY 33:27

I pray that my husband can do all things
through Christ who strengthens him.

PHILIPPIANS 4:13

I pray that my husband will wait on You,
LORD; that he will be of good courage,
and You shall strengthen his heart.

PSALM 27:14

I pray that my husband does not think it
strange concerning the fiery trial which
is to try him, as though some strange thing
happened to him; but that he will rejoice
to the extent that he partakes of Christ's
sufferings, that when His glory is
revealed, he may also be glad with
exceeding joy.

1 PETER 4:12–13

I pray that when my husband passes
through the waters, You will be with
him; and through the rivers, they shall not
overflow him. When he walks through
the fire, he shall not be burned, nor shall
the flame scorch him.

ISAIAH 43:2

I pray that while my husband's weeping
may endure for a night, joy comes to
him in the morning.

PSALM 30:5

I pray that my husband will be of good
courage, and that You shall strengthen
his heart, for his hope is in You, LORD.

PSALM 31:24

I pray that my husband shall obtain joy
and gladness and that sorrow and
sighing shall flee away.

ISAIAH 51:11

I pray that my husband will be anxious for
nothing, but in everything by prayer
and supplication, with thanksgiving, will
let his requests be made known to You,
God.

PHILIPPIANS 4:6

I pray that my husband will wait on You, LORD, and that he shall renew his strength. I pray that he shall mount up with wings like eagles; that he shall run and not be weary; that he shall walk and not faint.

ISAIAH 40:31

I pray that whatever things are true, whatever things are noble, whatever things are just, whatever things are pure, whatever things are lovely, whatever things are of good report, if there is any virtue and if there is anything praiseworthy—that my husband will meditate on these things.

PHILIPPIANS 4:8

7

DELIVERANCE

Lord Jesus, today, at this very moment, I ask You to deliver my husband from anything that is afflicting him in any way. Help him to know the truth that comes only from You and Your word and to be set free from all that is upon him. Thank You, Jesus, for freeing my husband and for filling him with joy and hope. Amen.

God, in accordance with Your Word...

I pray that my husband shall know the truth, and the truth shall make him free.

JOHN 8:32

——————— ◆ ———————

I pray that if You, Jesus, make my husband free, he shall be free indeed.

JOHN 8:36

I pray that there is therefore now no condemnation to my husband who is in Christ Jesus, who does not walk according to the flesh, but according to the Spirit. For the law of the Spirit of life in Christ Jesus has made him free from the law of sin and death.

ROMANS 8:1–2

I pray that my husband does not believe every spirit, but that he tests the spirits, whether they are of You, God; because many false prophets have gone out into the world. I pray that by this he will know the Spirit of God: that every spirit that confesses that Jesus Christ has come in the flesh is of God, and every spirit that does not confess that Jesus Christ has come in the flesh is not of God.

1 JOHN 4:1–3

I pray that He who is in my husband is greater than he who is in the world.

1 JOHN 4:4

I pray that my husband has overcome Satan
by the blood of the Lamb and by the
word of his testimony.

REVELATION 12:11

8
DEPRESSED

Lord God, I pray to You now as always in Jesus' name. I ask You now in His name to remove any depression that may come upon my husband at any time. Help him to know that if he will cry out to You that You will hear and deliver him. I pray Your word to You and I ask You to honor Your word and deliver him from any depression that he may ever experience. In Jesus' name, Amen.

God, in accordance
with Your Word...

I pray that my righteous husband will cry out, and You will hear and deliver him out of all of his troubles.

PSALM 34:17

---◆---

I pray, God, that You are the God of my husband's strength.

PSALM 43:2

I pray that while my husband's weeping
may endure for a night, his joy comes
in the morning.

PSALM 30:5

I pray that my husband will wait on You,
LORD. That he shall renew his strength.
That he shall mount up with wings like
eagles; that he shall run and not be
weary and that he shall walk and not faint.

ISAIAH 40:31

I pray, God, that you will comfort my
husband in all his tribulation, that he
may be able to comfort those who are in
any trouble, with the comfort with
which he himself is comforted by You.

2 CORINTHIANS 1:4

I pray that neither death nor life, nor angels
nor principalities nor powers, nor

things present nor things to come, nor height nor depth, nor any other created thing, shall be able to separate my husband from Your love, God, which is in Christ Jesus his Lord.

ROMANS 8:38–39

I pray that my husband does not think it strange concerning the fiery trial which is to try him, as though some strange thing happened to him; but that he will rejoice to the extent that he partakes of Christ's sufferings, so that when His glory is revealed, he may also be glad with exceeding joy.

1 PETER 4:12–13

I pray that whatever things are true, whatever things are noble, whatever things are just, whatever things are pure, whatever things are lovely, whatever things are of good report, if there is any virtue and if there is anything

praiseworthy—that my husband will
meditate on these things.

PHILIPPIANS 4:8

———◆———

I pray, God, that You will heal my husband's
broken heart and bind up his wounds.

PSALM 147:3

———◆———

I pray that my husband will fear not, for
You are with him. That he will not be
dismayed, for You are his God. I pray that
You will strengthen him; that You will
help him and that You will uphold him
with Your righteous right hand.

ISAIAH 41:10

———◆———

I pray that my husband will humble himself
under the mighty hand of God, that
You may exalt him in due time. I pray that

he will cast all his cares upon You, for
You care for him.

1 PETER 5:6–7

———————◆———————

I pray that my husband will always pray
and not lose heart.

LUKE 18:1

———————◆———————

I pray that my husband will not sorrow, for
the joy of the LORD is his strength.

NEHEMIAH 8:10

9
DESERTED BY LOVED ONES

Heavenly Father, I plead with You at this moment to honor Your word and set my husband on high. Your word has promised that You will never leave him or forsake him, no matter what his loved ones might do. He needs You now. Draw him close to You and carry his burdens for him. In the name of Your Son, Jesus, I pray. Amen.

God, in accordance
with Your Word...

I pray that because You have set Your love
upon my husband, You will deliver him.
You will set him on high, because he has
known Your name. I pray that he shall
call upon You and You will answer him.
That you will be with him in trouble.
That You will deliver him and honor him.
That with long life You will satisfy him
and show him Your salvation.

PSALM 91:14–16

I pray, God, that You will not forsake my
husband nor destroy him.

DEUTERONOMY 4:31

---◆---

I pray that You, God, will hear my husband
and that You will not forsake him.

ISAIAH 41:17

---◆---

I pray that my husband will cast all his
cares upon You, God, for You care for
him.

1 PETER 5:7

---◆---

I pray that while my husband is hard pressed
on every side, yet he is not crushed; he
is perplexed, but not in despair; persecuted,
but not forsaken; struck down, but not
destroyed—always carrying about in his
body the dying of the Lord Jesus, that

the life of Jesus also may be manifested in
his body.

2 CORINTHIANS 4:8–10

◆

I pray that my husband will no longer be
forsaken and You will delight in him.

ISAIAH 62:4

◆

I pray that my husband will be taught to
observe all things that Jesus has
commanded and that he knows that You
are with him always, even to the end
of the age.

MATTHEW 28:20

◆

I pray that because my husband knows
Your name, God, he will put his trust in
You; for You, LORD, have not forsaken those
who seek You.

PSALM 9:10

I pray that if my husband's father and his
mother forsake him that You will take
care of him.

PSALM 27:10

———◆———

I pray that my husband always remembers
that You will not forget him.

ISAIAH 49:15

———◆———

I pray that my husband's hope is in You,
God, and that he shall yet praise You,
the help of his countenance and his God.

PSALM 43:5

———◆———

I pray that my husband will be strong and
of good courage. That he will not fear
nor be afraid; for You, the LORD his God,
are the One who goes with him. I know
that You will not leave him or forsake him.

DEUTERONOMY 31:6

I pray that You will not forsake my husband,
for Your great name's sake, because it
has pleased You to make him one of Your
people.

1 SAMUEL 12:22

10

DISCOURAGED

Perfect God, in Jesus' name I ask You to remove from my husband any discouragement that he may be feeling at this time in his life. Teach him what Your word means when it says to wait on You and to be of good courage. Teach him that You will strengthen him. Thank You for hearing and honoring Your words. Amen.

God, in accordance
with Your Word ...

I pray that my husband will wait on You, LORD; that he will be of good courage and that You will strengthen his heart.

PSALM 27:14

───────◆───────

I pray that my husband will be of good courage and that You, God, shall strengthen his heart.

PSALM 31:24

I pray that my husband shall obtain joy
and gladness and that sorrow and sighing
shall flee away.

ISAIAH 51:11

I pray that my husband will not cast away
his confidence, which has great reward.
For he has need of endurance, so that after
he has done Your will, God, he may
receive his promise.

HEBREWS 10:35–36

I pray that my husband will not let his heart
be troubled. That he will believe in You,
God, and also in Jesus.

JOHN 14:1

I pray that my husband does not grow weary
while doing good, for in due season he
shall reap if he does not lose heart.

GALATIANS 6:9

I pray that my husband is confident of this
very thing, that You, God, who have
begun a good work in him will complete it
until the day of Jesus Christ.

PHILIPPIANS 1:6

———◆———

I pray that my husband will greatly rejoice,
though now for a little while, if need
be, he may be grieved by various trials. I
pray that the genuineness of his faith,
being much more precious than gold that
perishes, though it is tested by fire, may
be found to praise, honor, and glory at the
revelation of Jesus Christ, whom having
not seen, he loves. Though now he does
not see Him, yet believing, he rejoices
with joy inexpressible and full of glory,
receiving the end of his faith—the
salvation of his soul.

1 PETER 1:6–9

———◆———

I pray that in everything my husband will
be anxious for nothing, but in everything

by prayer and supplication, with
thanksgiving, lets his request be made
known to You, God; and Your peace, which
surpasses all understanding, will guard
his heart and mind through Christ Jesus.
And, God, whatever things are true,
whatever things are noble, whatever things
are just, whatever things are pure,
whatever things are lovely, whatever things
are of good report, if there is any virtue
and if there is anything praiseworthy—help
him to meditate on these things.

PHILIPPIANS 4:6–8

◆

I pray, God, though my husband walks in
the midst of trouble, You will revive
him. You will stretch out Your hand against
the wrath of his enemies. I pray that
with Your right hand You will save him.

PSALM 138:7

◆

I pray that my husband will always
understand and believe Your promise,
Jesus, that Your peace You left with him

and that Your peace You gave to him
and that not as the world gives did You
give it to him. Let not his heart be
troubled, neither let it be afraid.

JOHN 14:27

I pray that while my husband is hard pressed
on every side, he is not crushed, he is
perplexed, but not in despair; persecuted,
but not forsaken; struck down, but not
destroyed—always carrying about in his
body the dying of the Lord Jesus, that
the life of Jesus also may be manifested in
his body.

2 CORINTHIANS 4:8–10

11

DISSATISFIED

Lord Jesus, through the power of Your perfect and error-free word, I call upon You to replace any dissatisfaction in my husband's life with joy, hope and happiness. Your word says his soul will be satisfied and he shall have every good thing. Through my faith and the authority of Your word I now pray Your word for my husband and ask that You hear and honor these words. Thank You for hearing my prayers. Amen.

God, in accordance
with Your Word...

I pray that my husband can do all things through Christ who strengthens him.

PHILIPPIANS 4:13

I pray that my husband will be satisfied with good by the fruit of his mouth.

PROVERBS 12:14

I pray that my husband's soul shall be
satisfied as with marrow and fatness,
and his mouth shall praise You with joyful
lips.

PSALM 63:5

———————◆———————

I pray that my husband will bless You, Lord,
with all that is within him and that he
will forget not all Your benefits. I pray that
he will not forget who forgives all his
iniquities and who heals all his diseases. I
pray that he will not forget who redeems
his life from destruction and who crowns
him with lovingkindness and tender
mercies and who satisfies his mouth with
good things, so that his youth is renewed
like the eagle's.

PSALM 103:1–5

———————◆———————

I pray, God, that You will satisfy my husband's
longing soul and fill his hungry soul
with goodness.

PSALM 107:9

I pray that because my husband seeks You,
LORD, he shall not lack any good thing.

PSALM 34:10

I pray that my husband will delight himself
in You, LORD, and You shall give him
the desires of his heart.

PSALM 37:4

I pray that my husband will trust and not
be afraid; for You, God, are his strength
and his song. You have become his salvation.

ISAIAH 12:2

I pray that You, God, who supply seed to
the sower and bread for food, will
supply and multiply the seed my husband
has sown and will increase the fruits of
his righteousness.

2 CORINTHIANS 9:10

12

DISTRESS / SADNESS

God in heaven, You have promised the comfort of the Holy Spirit to us in times such as this. I ask You for a special comforting for my husband. Your word says that while sadness may come upon him that his joy will return in the morning. I pray this, Your word, for my husband. Remove his distress. Take his sadness. And honor these Your words that I am about to pray. Thank You in Jesus' name. Amen.

God, in accordance
with Your Word...

I pray that my husband has done justice
and righteousness and that You will
not leave him to his oppressors.

PSALM 119:121

I pray that You, God, will strengthen my
husband according to Your word.

PSALM 119:28

I pray that while my husband may be despised, he does not forget Your precepts.

PSALM 119:141

I pray that while trouble and anguish have overtaken my husband, Your commandments are his delights. The righteousness of Your testimonies is everlasting. I pray that You will give him understanding, and he shall live.

PSALM 119:143–144

I pray that it is good for my husband that he has been afflicted so that he can learn Your statutes.

PSALM 119:71

I pray that You, God, will consider my husband's affliction and deliver him, for he does not forget Your law. I pray that

You will plead his cause and redeem him. Revive him according to Your word.

PSALM 119:153–154

———◆———

I pray that in righteousness my husband shall be established. That he shall be far from oppression, for he shall not fear; and from terror, for it shall not come near him.

ISAIAH 54:14

———◆———

I pray that my husband has great peace because he loves Your law, God, and nothing causes him to stumble.

PSALM 119:165

———◆———

I pray that if my husband has gone astray like a lost sheep, that You, God, will seek him, Your servant, and not let him forget Your commandments.

PSALM 119:176

I pray that my husband will always pray
"Blessed be the LORD," who daily loads
him with benefits.

PSALM 68:19

---◆---

I pray, God, that You will bring my husband
up out of a horrible pit and out of the
miry clay. Set his feet upon a rock and
establish his steps.

PSALM 40:2

---◆---

I pray that You, God, are my husband's
refuge and strength, a very present help
in trouble and that he will not fear.

PSALM 46:1–2

---◆---

I pray that since Your name, LORD, is a
strong tower, that my righteous
husband runs to it and is safe.

PROVERBS 18:10

I pray that my husband will not let his heart
be troubled and that he will always
believe in God and in Jesus.

JOHN 14:1

————◆————

I pray that my husband will not sorrow, for
the joy of the LORD is his strength.

NEHEMIAH 8:10

————◆————

I pray that my husband will always live
with the realization that his Lord is
faithful and will establish him and guard
him from the evil one.

2 THESSALONIANS 3:3

13

DON'T UNDERSTAND GOD

Lord God, the words that I am about to pray are
Your words. Hear them, please, and honor them.
Help my husband to understand that because Your
thoughts are often higher than his thoughts that he
may not always understand Your thoughts and
Your way. Remind him of Your promise that if he
will call upon You, You will tell him great and
unsearchable things that he does not know. I now
pray Your word to You in Jesus' name. Amen.

God, in accordance
with Your Word...

I pray that You, God, will help my husband
to understand that Your thoughts are
not his thoughts nor are his ways Your ways.
That he will understand that as the
heavens are higher than the earth, so are
Your ways higher than his ways and
Your thoughts higher than his thoughts.

ISAIAH 55:8–9

I pray that my husband will call to You, God, and that You will answer him and show him great and mighty things, which he does not know.

JEREMIAH 33:3

I pray that if You, God, are for my husband, who can be against him?

ROMANS 8:31

I pray that in all things my husband is more than a conqueror through Him who loved him.

ROMANS 8:37

I pray that as for You, God, Your way is perfect. The word of the LORD is proven; You are a shield to my husband who trusts in You.

PSALM 18:30

I pray that my husband will pursue the knowledge of the LORD.

HOSEA 6:3

———————◆———————

I pray, God, that You will perfect that which concerns my husband and that your mercy, O LORD, endures forever.

PSALM 138:8

———————◆———————

I pray that You, God, will make an everlasting covenant with my husband, that You will not turn away from doing him good; but that You will put Your fear in his heart so that he will not depart from You.

JEREMIAH 32:40

———————◆———————

I pray that my husband will cast his burden on You, LORD, and You shall sustain him.

PSALM 55:22

I pray that my husband will hold fast the confession of his hope without wavering, for You, God, who promised are faithful.

HEBREWS 10:23

———————◆———————

I pray that all things work together for good to my husband who loves You, God, to him who was called according to Your purpose.

ROMANS 8:28

———————◆———————

I pray that my husband does not think it strange concerning the fiery trial which is to try him, as though some strange thing happened to him. But that he will rejoice to the extent that He partakes of Christ's sufferings, that when His glory is revealed, he may also be glad with exceeding joy.

1 PETER 4:12–13

I pray that no temptation has overtaken
my husband except such as is common
to man; but You, God, are faithful, who
will not allow him to be tempted beyond
what he is able, but with the temptation
You will also make the way of escape,
that he may be able to bear it.

1 CORINTHIANS 10:13

I pray that while many are the afflictions of
the righteous husband, You, LORD deliver
him out of them all.

PSALM 34:19

I pray that my husband will fear not, for
You, God, are with him. That he will
not be dismayed, for You are his God. That
You will strengthen him and help him.
That You will uphold him with Your
righteous right hand.

ISAIAH 41:10

14

DOUBTING GOD

Heavenly Father, today I pray the power of Your perfect word to remove any doubts about You that my husband might have. Your word says that Your way is perfect and Your word is proven. May the Holy Spirit impart Your perfection to my husband and remove any doubts that he may have now or at any time in his life. Help him more than ever before to believe and not doubt. And it is in Jesus' name that I pray. Amen.

God, in accordance with Your Word...

I pray that You, LORD, are not slack concerning Your promise, as some count slackness, but are longsuffering toward my husband, not willing that he should perish but that he should come to repentance.

2 PETER 3:9

I pray that because Your way is perfect and
Your word is proven; that You, God,
are a shield to my husband who trusts in
You.

PSALM 18:30

I pray, God, that my husband will always
remember that Your hand is not
shortened so that it cannot save; nor Your
ear heavy, that it cannot hear.

ISAIAH 59:1

I pray that my husband knows that He who
calls him is faithful, who also will do it.

1 THESSALONIANS 5:24

I pray that my husband does not seek what
he should eat or what he should drink,
nor have an anxious mind. For all these
things the nations of the world seek
after, and You, his Father, knows that he

needs these things. I pray that he will
seek the kingdom of God, and all these
things shall be added to him.

LUKE 12:29–31

———————◆———————

I pray, God, that my husband is aware that
You have said Your counsel shall stand
and You will do all Your pleasure. Indeed,
You have spoken it and You will also
bring it to pass. You have purposed it and
You will also do it.

ISAIAH 46:10–11

———————◆———————

I pray that my husband does not think it
strange concerning the fiery trial which
is to try him, as though some strange thing
happened to him. But that he rejoices
to the extent that he partakes of Christ's
sufferings, that when His glory is
revealed, he may also be glad with
exceeding joy.

1 PETER 4:12–13

I pray that whatever things my husband asks for when he prays, that he will believe that he will receive them, and he will have them.

MARK 11:24

I pray that my husband will always remember that You, God, have declared that, "So shall My word be that goes forth from My mouth. It shall not return to Me void. But it shall accomplish what I please, and it shall prosper in the thing for which I sent it."

ISAIAH 55:11

I pray that my husband knows that faith comes by hearing and hearing by the word of God.

ROMANS 10:17

15

EMOTIONALLY UPSET

Jesus, I am here to pray Your word and to ask You to give great peace to my husband because he loves You so much. As Your word says, give him a sound mind and a peace that passes all understanding. In accordance with Your word let him be anxious for nothing. Thank you, Jesus, for honoring Your word in this important time in my husband's life. Amen.

God, in accordance
with Your Word...

I pray that my husband will have great peace because he loves Your law and nothing causes him to stumble.

PSALM 119:165

---◆---

I pray that You, God, will heal my husband's broken heart and bind up his wounds.

PSALM 147:3

I pray that because my husband believes
in You, God, he will by no means be
put to shame.

1 PETER 2:6

———————◆———————

I pray that You, God, will help my husband;
therefore he will not be disgraced. He
can set his face like a flint and know that
he will not be ashamed.

ISAIAH 50:7

———————◆———————

I pray that my husband will cast his burden
on You, LORD, and that You will sustain
him.

PSALM 55:22

———————◆———————

I pray that my husband will be anxious for
nothing, but in everything by prayer
and supplication, with thanksgiving, will
let his requests be made known to You,

God, and Your peace, God, which surpasses
all understanding, will guard his heart
and mind through Christ Jesus.

PHILIPPIANS 4:6–7

———◆———

I pray that You, God, have not given my
husband a spirit of fear, but of power
and of love and of a sound mind.

2 TIMOTHY 1:7

———◆———

I pray that my husband will realize that
You, God, are not the author of confusion
but of peace.

1 CORINTHIANS 14:33

———◆———

I pray that my husband knows that where
envy and self-seeking exist, confusion
and every evil thing will be there. I pray
that he will also know that the wisdom
that is from above is first pure, then

I pray that my husband will fear not, for
You, God, are with him. That he be not
dismayed, for You are his God. I pray that
You will strengthen him and help him
and that You will uphold him with Your
righteous right hand.

ISAIAH 41:10

I pray that my husband knows that where
envy and self-seeking exist, confusion
and every evil thing will be there. I pray
that he will also know that the wisdom
that is from above is first pure, then
peaceable, gentle, willing to yield, full
of mercy and good fruits, without partiality
and without hypocrisy and that the fruit
of righteousness is sown in peace by those
who make peace.

JAMES 3:16–18

I pray that when my husband passes through
the waters, You, God, will be with him.
And when he passes through the rivers,

they shall not overflow him. I pray that
when he walks through the fire, he shall
not be burned, nor shall the flame scorch
him. You are the LORD his God.

ISAIAH 43:2–3

I pray that while my husband's weeping
may endure for a night, his joy comes
in the morning.

PSALM 30:5

I pray that You, God, will comfort my
husband in all his tribulation, that he
may be able to comfort those who are in
any trouble, with the comfort with
which he himself is comforted by You.

2 CORINTHIANS 1:4

I pray that whatever things are true,
whatever things are noble, whatever
things are just, whatever things are pure,

whatever things are lovely, whatever
things are of good report, if there is any
virtue and if there is anything
praiseworthy—that my husband will
meditate on these things.

PHILIPPIANS 4:8

I pray that neither death nor life, nor angels
nor principalities nor powers, nor things
present nor things to come, nor height nor
depth, nor any other created thing,
shall be able to separate my husband from
the love of God which is in Christ Jesus
his Lord.

ROMANS 8:38–39

16

FAITH

Father God, in the name of Your Son, Jesus, I pray to You Your perfect word for my husband. Increase his faith. Help him to remember that You said he is to walk by faith and not by sight. Hear and answer Your word now concerning my husband's faith. Thank You in Jesus' name. Amen.

God, in accordance with Your Word...

I pray that You, Lord, will increase my husband's faith.

LUKE 17:5

———◆———

I pray that my husband's faith comes by hearing, and hearing by the word of God.

ROMANS 10:17

I pray that my husband will walk by faith
and not by sight.

2 CORINTHIANS 5:7

I pray that my husband will have a pure
heart, a good conscience, and sincere
faith.

1 TIMOTHY 1:5

I pray that my husband will always
remember that faith is the substance of
things hoped for and the evidence of things
not seen.

HEBREWS 11:1

I pray that my husband remembers that
faith by itself, if it does not have works,
is dead.

JAMES 2:17

I pray that my husband will constantly take the shield of faith with which he will be able to quench all the fiery darts of the wicked one.

EPHESIANS 6:16

I pray that my husband will put on the breastplate of faith and love, and as his helmet the hope of salvation.

1 THESSALONIANS 5:8

I pray that my husband will always have faith and a good conscience.

1 TIMOTHY 1:19

I pray that my husband will fight the good fight of faith, that he will lay hold on eternal life, to which he was also called.

1 TIMOTHY 6:12

I pray my husband will draw near with a
true heart in the full assurance of his
faith and that he will have his heart sprinkled
from an evil conscience and his body
washed with pure water.

HEBREWS 10:22

I pray that my husband understands that
without faith it is impossible to please
You, God, and that for him to come to You
he must believe that You are and that
You are a rewarder of those who diligently
seek You.

HEBREWS 11:6

I pray that my husband will count all things
as a loss for the excellence of the
knowledge of Christ Jesus his Lord, for
whom he has suffered the loss of all
things, and count them as rubbish, that he
may gain Christ and be found in Him,
not having his own righteousness, which is
from the law, but that which is through

faith in Christ, the righteousness which is
from God by faith; that he may know
Him and the power of His resurrection,
and the fellowship of His sufferings,
being conformed to His death.

PHILIPPIANS 3:8–10

I pray that my husband will be just and
will live by faith.

HABAKKUK 2:4

I pray that my husband will remember that
Abraham believed God, and it was
accounted to him for righteousness.

ROMANS 4:3

I pray that my husband, having been justified
by faith, will have peace with You, God,
through his Lord Jesus Christ.

ROMANS 5:1

I pray that my husband will be just and will live by faith.

HEBREWS 10:38

I pray that my husband shall believe in You, the LORD his God, and he shall be established. I pray also that he will believe Your prophets and he shall prosper.

2 CHRONICLES 20:20

I pray that according to my husband's faith, it will be to him.

MATTHEW 9:29

I pray that my husband will have faith as a mustard seed and he will say to his mountain, "Move from here to there," and it will move and nothing will be impossible to him.

MATTHEW 17:20

I pray that my husband will have faith in
You, God.

MARK 11:22

---◆---

I pray for my husband the righteousness of
You, God, which is through faith in Jesus
Christ on he who believes.

ROMANS 3:22

---◆---

I pray, God, that in Your forbearance You
have passed over my husband's sins
that were previously committed.

ROMANS 3:25

---◆---

I pray that my husband will remember that
if he has the gift of prophecy, and
understands all mysteries and all
knowledge, and though he has all faith,
so that he can remove mountains, but has
not love, he is nothing.

1 CORINTHIANS 13:2

I pray that my husband will watch and that
he will stand fast in the faith and that
he will be brave and strong.

1 CORINTHIANS 16:13

I pray that my husband will examine himself
as to whether he is in the faith and that
he will test himself.

2 CORINTHIANS 13:5

I pray that my husband knows that he is
not justified by the works of the law
but by faith in Jesus Christ.

GALATIANS 2:16

I pray that my husband has been crucified
with Christ. That it is no longer he who
lives, but Christ who lives in him. And that
the life which he now lives in the flesh

he lives by faith in the Son of God, who
loves him and gave Himself for him.

GALATIANS 2:20

———◆———

I pray that my husband knows the Holy
Scriptures, which are able to make him
wise for salvation through his faith which
is in Christ Jesus.

2 TIMOTHY 3:15

———◆———

I pray that my husband will fight the good
fight; that he will finish the race; and
that he will keep the faith.

2 TIMOTHY 4:7

———◆———

I pray that the sharing of my husband's
faith may become effective by the
acknowledgment of every good thing which
is in Christ Jesus.

PHILEMON 1:6

I pray that my husband understands that
as the body without the spirit is dead,
so faith without works is dead also.

JAMES 2:26

I pray that my husband will realize that if
he does not believe he shall not be
established.

ISAIAH 7:9

I pray that it is by faith that my husband
understands that the worlds were framed
by the word of God, so that the things
which are seen were not made of things
which are visible.

HEBREWS 11:3

I pray that my husband will always look
unto Jesus, the author and finisher of
his faith, who for the joy that was set

before Him endured the cross, despising
the shame, and has sat down at the right
hand of the throne of God.

HEBREWS 12:2

17

FEAR

God, I pray Your word to You now to remove any and all fears that my husband may be harboring either now or in the future. I ask You to remember that my prayers are actually Your words on the subject of fear. Please honor Your perfect and error-free word and remove any and all fears now and forever in my husband. Thank You, God, for hearing my prayers, in Jesus' name. Amen.

God, in accordance
with Your Word...

I pray that Your truth, God, shall be my husband's shield and buckler and that he shall not be afraid.

PSALM 91:4–5

I pray that no evil shall befall my husband.

PSALM 91:10

I pray that my husband will not be afraid
of sudden terror, nor of trouble from
the wicked when it comes. I pray that You,
LORD, will be his confidence and will
keep his foot from being caught.

PROVERBS 3:25–26

I pray that in righteousness my husband
shall be established. He shall be far from
oppression, for he shall not fear. And from
terror, for it shall not come near him.

ISAIAH 54:14

I pray that in You, God, my husband has
put his trust and that he will not be
afraid.

PSALM 56:11

I pray that You, LORD, are my husband's
helper and that he will not fear.

HEBREWS 13:6

I pray that my husband knows that You, God, have not given him a spirit of fear, but of power and of love and of a sound mind.

2 TIMOTHY 1:7

———————◆———————

I pray that my husband did not receive the spirit of bondage again to fear, but that he received the Spirit of adoption by whom he cries out, "Abba, Father."

ROMANS 8:15

———————◆———————

I pray that in my husband there is no fear in love; because perfect love casts out fear.

1 JOHN 4:18

———————◆———————

I pray that You, God, will give Your angels charge over my husband, to keep him in all his ways.

PSALM 91:11

I pray that though my husband walks through the valley of the shadow of death, he will fear no evil; for You, God, are with him. Your rod and Your staff, they comfort him.

PSALM 23:4

I pray that my husband will be of good courage and that You, God, shall strengthen his heart for his hope is in the LORD.

PSALM 31:24

I pray that if You, God, are for my husband, who can be against him? Who shall separate him from the love of Christ? Shall tribulation, or distress, or persecution, or famine, or nakedness, or peril, or sword? I pray that in all these things he is more than a conqueror through Him who loved him. For I am persuaded that neither death nor life, nor angels nor principalities nor powers, nor things present nor things

to come, nor height nor depth, nor any
other created thing, shall be able to
separate my husband from Your love, God,
which is in Christ Jesus his Lord.

ROMANS 8:31, 35, 37–39

◆

I pray that my husband receives the peace
that You, Jesus, have left with him, the
peace You gave to him. Let not his heart
be troubled, neither let it be afraid.

JOHN 14:27

◆

I pray that You, LORD, are my husband's
light and his salvation. Whom shall he
fear? Though an army may encamp against
him, his heart shall not fear. In this he
will be confident.

PSALM 27:1, 3

18
FINANCIAL PROBLEMS

Heavenly Father, it is not Your will that my husband should have to contend unnecessarily with financial problems. Because I believe strongly in Your word, I present to You as my prayers for my husband Your very words on this subject. Please honor Your word and release him from any and all financial problems in his life. I pray Your words in Jesus' name. Amen.

God, in accordance
with Your Word...

I pray that my husband may prosper in all things and be in health, just as his soul prospers.

3 JOHN 1:2

I pray that You, LORD, are my husband's shepherd and that he shall not want.

PSALM 23:1

I pray that my husband will seek You, LORD, and not lack any good thing.

PSALM 34:10

———————◆———————

I pray that all these blessings shall come upon my husband and overtake him, because he obeys the voice of the LORD his God. He shall be blessed in the city and he shall be blessed in the country. He shall be blessed when he comes in and he shall be blessed when he goes out. I pray that You, LORD, will command Your blessing on him in his storehouses and in all to which he sets his hand.

DEUTERONOMY 28:2–3, 6–8

———————◆———————

I pray that my husband will give, and it will be given to him: good measure, pressed down, shaken together, and running over will be put into his bosom. For with the same measure that he uses, it will be measured back to him.

LUKE 6:38

I pray that because freely my husband has received, freely he will give.

MATTHEW 10:8

———◆———

I pray that on the first day of the week my husband will lay something aside, storing up as he may prosper, so that he may give to those in need.

1 CORINTHIANS 16:2

———◆———

I pray that my husband realizes that if he sows sparingly he will also reap sparingly and he who sows bountifully he will also reap bountifully. I pray that he will give as he purposes in his heart, not grudgingly or of necessity; for You, God, love a cheerful giver. And You are able to make all grace abound toward him, that my husband, always having all sufficiency in all things, may have an abundance for every good work.

2 CORINTHIANS 9:6–8

I pray that my husband will bring all his tithes into the storehouse, that there may be food in God's house. And that he will try You, God, in this and see if You will not open for him the windows of heaven and pour out for him such blessing that there will not be room enough to receive it.

MALACHI 3:10

I pray that my husband will remember that everyone who has left houses or brothers or sisters or father or mother or wife or children or lands, for Your name's sake, Lord, shall receive a hundredfold, and inherit eternal life. I pray also that he will remember that many who are first will be last and the last first.

MATTHEW 19:29–30

I pray that this Book of the Law shall not depart from my husband's mouth, but he shall meditate in it day and night, that

he may observe to do according to all
that is written in it. For then he will make
his way prosperous, and then he will
have good success.

JOSHUA 1:8

———◆———

I pray, God, that you will give wisdom and
knowledge and joy to my husband who
is good in Your sight. But to the sinner You
will give the work of gathering and
collecting, that he may give to my husband
who is good before You.

ECCLESIASTES 2:26

———◆———

I pray that my husband leaves an
inheritance to his children's children.

PROVERBS 13:22

———◆———

I pray that my husband does not worry,
saying, "What shall I eat?" or "What shall
I drink?" or "What shall I wear?" For You,

his Heavenly Father, know that he needs
all these things. But I pray that he will
seek first Your kingdom, God, and Your
righteousness, and all these things shall be
added to him. I also pray that he does
not worry about tomorrow, for tomorrow
will worry about its own things.

MATTHEW 6:25, 33–34

I pray that You, God, shall supply all my
husband's needs according to Your
riches in glory by Christ Jesus.

PHILIPPIANS 4:19

19

FORGIVENESS

Lord God, for reasons known to You, my husband needs Your forgiveness. Because I sense that and know that he has need of Your forgiveness I come to You today, praying Your very words back to You in order that he might be forgiven. Bless now the very words from Your mouth on my husband's behalf. Thank You now in Jesus' name. Amen.

God, in accordance
with Your Word...

I pray that as far as the east is from the west, so far have You, God, removed my husband's transgressions from him.

PSALM 103:12

I pray that my husband's transgressions are forgiven and his sin is covered.

PSALM 32:1

I pray that in You, Jesus, my husband has
redemption through Your blood, the
forgiveness of his sins, according to the
riches of God's grace which He made
to abound toward him in all wisdom and
prudence, having made known to him
the mystery of His will, according to His
good pleasure which He purposed in
Himself.

EPHESIANS 1:7–9

I pray, God, that it is You who blots out my
husband's transgressions for Your own
sake and that You will not remember his
sins.

ISAIAH 43:25

I pray that my husband will return to You,
LORD, and that You will have mercy on
him; and to his God, for You will abundantly
pardon.

ISAIAH 55:7

I pray that my husband will bear with others,
and forgive others, if he has a
complaint against any others, even as
Christ forgave him, so he also must do.

COLOSSIANS 3:13

I pray that because my husband is in Christ,
he is a new creation. The old things
have passed away and all things have
become new.

2 CORINTHIANS 5:17

I pray that if my husband confesses his
sins, that You, God, are faithful and just
to forgive his sins and to cleanse him from
all unrighteousness.

1 JOHN 1:9

I pray that You, God, will cleanse my
husband from all his iniquity by which
he has sinned against You, and that You

will pardon all his iniquities by which
he has sinned and by which he has
transgressed against You.

JEREMIAH 33:8

I pray that whenever my husband stands
praying, if he has anything against
anyone that he will forgive them, so that
You, his Father in heaven, may also
forgive him of his trespasses.

MARK 11:25

I pray that if my husband sins, he has an
Advocate with You, the Father, Jesus
Christ the righteous.

1 JOHN 2:1

20

GODLY LIFE

Lord Jesus, my Lord and my Savior, more than anything else I desire that my wonderful husband will live a godly life in Your sight. Your words are my prayers to You on his behalf. Please honor them by keeping my husband in the center of Your will in all that he does. Thank You for all that You do and especially for honoring this my prayer. Amen.

God, in accordance
with Your Word...

I pray that if my husband believes on You, Jesus, who justifies the ungodly, his faith is accounted for righteousness.

ROMANS 4:5

I pray that what the law could not do in my husband in that it was weak through the flesh, You, God, did by sending Your

own Son in the likeness of sinful flesh,
on account of sin: You condemned sin in
my husband, that the righteous
requirement of the law might be fulfilled
in he who does not walk according to
the flesh but according to the Spirit.

ROMANS 8:3–4

I pray that my husband does not present
his members as instruments of
unrighteousness to sin, but presents himself
to You, God, as being alive from the
dead, and his members as instruments of
righteousness to You. For sin shall not
have dominion over him, for he is not
under law but under grace.

ROMANS 6:13–14

I pray that if my husband lives, he lives to
You, Lord; and if he dies, he dies to
You, Lord. Therefore, whether he lives or
dies, he is Yours, Lord.

ROMANS 14:8

I pray that my husband will present his body as a living sacrifice, holy, and acceptable to You, God.

ROMANS 12:1

I pray that my husband will not think of himself more highly than he ought to think, but to think soberly, as You, God, have dealt to him a measure of faith.

ROMANS 12:3

I pray that because You, Christ, are in my husband, his body is dead because of sin, but the Spirit is life because of righteousness.

ROMANS 8:10

I pray that my husband will not be conformed to this world, but that he will be transformed by the renewing of his mind, that he may prove what is that

good and acceptable and perfect will of
God.

ROMANS 12:2

I pray that my husband whom You, God,
predestined, You also called; he whom
You called, You also justified; and he whom
You justified, You also glorified.

ROMANS 8:30

I pray that because my husband is in You,
Christ, he is a new creation; old things
have passed away, behold, all things have
become new.

2 CORINTHIANS 5:17

I pray that You, God, made Jesus who knew
no sin to be sin for my husband, that
he might become the righteousness of You
in Him.

2 CORINTHIANS 5:21

I pray that You, God, are able to make all grace abound toward my husband, that he, always having all sufficiency in all things, may have an abundance for every good work.

2 CORINTHIANS 9:8

I pray that if my husband glories, he will glory in You, LORD.

1 CORINTHIANS 1:31

I pray that my husband will not let sin reign in his mortal body, that he should obey it in its lusts.

ROMANS 6:12

I pray that my husband will remember that his body is the temple of the Holy Spirit who is in him, whom he has from You, God. And that he is not his own for he

was bought at a price. Therefore, I pray
that he will glorify God in his body and
in his spirit, which are Yours, God.

1 CORINTHIANS 6:19–20

———◆———

I pray that my husband has been set free
from sin and has become a slave of
God.

ROMANS 6:22

———◆———

I pray that it is good for my husband to
draw near to You, God; to put his trust
in the LORD God, that he may declare all
Your works.

PSALM 73:28

———◆———

I pray that my husband will be renewed in
the spirit of his mind and that he will
put on his new self which was created

according to You, God, in true
righteousness and holiness.

EPHESIANS 4:23–24

I pray that my husband will delight himself
in You, LORD, and that You shall give
him the desires of his heart.

PSALM 37:4

I pray that You, God, will satisfy my
husband's mouth with good things so
that his youth is renewed like the eagle's.

PSALM 103:5

I pray that You, God, are a companion to
my husband who fears You and keeps
Your precepts.

PSALM 119:63

I pray that my husband's ways are directed
to keep Your statutes, God.

PSALM 119:5

I pray that my husband will cleanse his
way by taking heed according to Your
word, God.

PSALM 119:9

I pray that with my husband's whole heart
he has sought You, God. Let him not
wander from Your commandments.

PSALM 119:10

I pray that my husband has hidden Your
word in his heart, God, that he might
not sin against You.

PSALM 119:11

I pray that my husband, who walks in the law of the LORD, will be blessed.

PSALM 119:1

I pray that my husband will delight himself in Your statutes, God, and that he will not forget Your word.

PSALM 119:16

I pray that You, God, will open my husband's eyes, that he may see wondrous things from Your law.

PSALM 119:18

I pray that my husband has chosen the way of truth and that Your judgments he has laid before him. I pray that he will cling to Your testimonies, God, and that he will not be put to shame.

PSALM 119:30–31

I pray that my husband has declared his
ways and that You, God, have answered
him and that You will teach him Your
statutes.

PSALM 119:26

◆

I pray that You, God, will make my husband
understand the way of Your precepts;
so shall he meditate on Your wondrous
works.

PSALM 119:27

◆

I pray, God, that Your testimonies also are
my husband's delight and his counselors.

PSALM 119:24

◆

I pray, God, that You will make my husband
walk in the path of Your commandments
and that he will delight in it.

PSALM 119:35

I pray that my husband will incline his heart
to Your testimonies, God, and not to
covetousness. I pray that he will turn away
his eyes from looking at worthless things
and that You will revive him in Your way.

PSALM 119:36–37

I pray that You, God, will remember the
word to my husband, Your servant,
upon which You have caused him to hope.

PSALM 119:49

I pray that You, God, will be merciful to
my husband according to Your word.

PSALM 119:58

I pray, O God, that my husband has thought
about his ways and has turned his feet
to Your testimonies. I pray that he has made

haste, and did not delay to keep Your
commandments.

PSALM 119:59–60

I pray that You, God, will teach my husband
good judgment and knowledge, for he
believes Your commandments.

PSALM 119:66

I pray, God, that Your hands have made my
husband and fashioned him. Give him
understanding that he may learn Your
commandments.

PSALM 119:76

I pray, God, that You will let my husband's
heart be blameless regarding Your
statutes, that he may not be ashamed.

PSALM 119:80

I pray that You, God, will give my husband understanding that he may know Your testimonies.

PSALM 119:125

I pray, Lord God, that my husband will never forget Your precepts, for by them You have given him life.

PSALM 119:93

I pray that Your Word, O God, is a lamp to my husband's feet and a light to his path.

PSALM 119:105

I pray that You, God, are my husband's hiding place and his shield and that his hope is in Your word.

PSALM 119:114

I pray, God, that You will let Your merciful
kindness be for my husband's comfort.

PSALM 119:76

I pray that my husband's steps are directed
by Your word, God, and that You let no
iniquity have dominion over him.

PSALM 119:133

I pray that my husband shall love You, the
LORD his God, with all his heart, with
all his soul, with all his mind, and with all
his strength and that he shall love his
neighbor as himself.

MARK 12:30–31

I pray that You, Jesus, are always at my
husband's right hand, that he may not
be shaken.

ACTS 2:25

141

I pray that my husband may gain You, Christ, and be found in You, not having his own righteousness, which is from the law, but that which is through faith in You, the righteousness which is from God by faith; that he may know You and the power of Your resurrection, and the fellowship of Your sufferings, being conformed to Your death.

PHILIPPIANS 3:8–10

I pray that if my husband confesses his sins, that You, God, are faithful and just to forgive his sins and to cleanse him from all unrighteousness.

1 JOHN 1:9

I pray that the work of my husband's righteousness will be peace, and the effect of his righteousness, quietness and assurance forever.

ISAIAH 32:17

I pray that blessed is my husband who
walks not in the counsel of the ungodly,
nor stands in the path of sinners, nor sits
in the seat of the scornful. But his
delight is in the law of the LORD, and in
Your law he meditates day and night. I
pray that he shall be like a tree planted by
the rivers of water that brings forth its
fruit in its season, whose leaf also shall not
wither; and whatever he does shall
prosper.

PSALM 1:1–3

I pray that my husband shall know the truth
and the truth shall make him free.

JOHN 8:32

I pray that my husband takes up Your
whole armor, God, that he may be able
to withstand in the evil day, and having
done all, to stand. I pray that he will
gird his waist with truth, that he will put on
the breastplate of righteousness and

will shoe his feet with the preparation of
the gospel of peace and above all, take
the shield of faith with which he will be
able to quench all the fiery darts of the
wicked one. I pray that he will take the
helmet of salvation, and the sword of
the Spirit, which is the word of God;
praying always with all prayer and
supplication in the Spirit, being watchful
to this end with all perseverance and
supplication for all the saints.

EPHESIANS 6:13–18

I pray that my husband will be diligent to
present himself approved to You, God,
a worker who does not need to be ashamed,
rightly dividing the word of truth.

2 TIMOTHY 2:15

I pray that no one deceives my husband
with empty words.

EPHESIANS 5:6

I pray that my husband will be a doer of
the word and not a hearer only.

JAMES 1:22

◆

I pray that my husband will not be deceived
for You, God, are not mocked; for
whatever he sows, that he will also reap.

GALATIANS 6:7

◆

I pray that my husband always remembers
that all Scripture is given by inspiration
of You, God, and is profitable for doctrine,
for reproof, for correction, for
instruction in righteousness, that the man
of God may be complete, thoroughly
equipped for every good work.

2 TIMOTHY 3:16–17

21

GOD'S LOVE

Lord God, I pray Your words to You as my way to ask You to love my husband in a very special way. Help him, Lord, to experience Your love through Your word and through other ways as well. Thank You, Father, in Jesus' name. Amen.

God, in accordance with Your Word...

I pray that my husband knows that love is not that he loved You, God, but that You loved him and sent Your Son to be the propitiation for his sins.

1 JOHN 4:10

I pray that my husband loves You, God, because You first loved him.

1 JOHN 4:19

I pray that You, Christ, may dwell in my
husband's heart through faith and that
he, being rooted and grounded in love,
may be able to comprehend with all
the saints what is the width and length and
depth and height—to know Your love
which passes knowledge; that he may be
filled with all the fullness of God.

EPHESIANS 3:17–19

———◆———

I pray that my husband never forgets that
You, God, demonstrated Your own love
toward him, in that while he was still a
sinner, Christ died for him.

ROMANS 5:8

———◆———

I pray that neither death nor life, nor
angels nor principalities nor powers,
nor things present nor things to come, nor
height nor depth, nor any other
created thing, shall be able to separate my

husband from the love of You, God,
which is in Christ Jesus his Lord.

ROMANS 8:38–39

I pray that You, God, so loved my husband
that You gave Your only begotten Son,
that my husband who believes in Him
should not perish but have everlasting
life.

JOHN 3:16

I pray that my husband has Your
commandments, Jesus, and keeps them
and loves You. And because he loves You
will be loved by God, and You will love
him and manifest Yourself to him.

JOHN 14:21

I pray that my husband knows that You,
God, have loved him with an

everlasting love and with lovingkindness
You have drawn him.

JEREMIAH 31:3

I pray that my husband realizes that You,
God, will rejoice over him with
gladness. That You will quiet him in your
love and that You will rejoice over him
with singing.

ZEPHANIAH 3:17

22
GOD'S WORD

Heavenly Father, Your word is such an important part of my life. I pray that it will be the same in my husband's life and that Your word will be living and sharper than any two-edged sword in his life. I'm praying Your words that Your word may be important to him. Thank You, Father, in Jesus' name for hearing and answering my prayers for my husband. Amen.

God, in accordance
with Your Word...

I pray, God, that in my husband's life Your
word is living and powerful, and
sharper than any two-edged sword,
piercing even to the division of his
soul, spirit, and of his joints and marrow,
and that it is a discerner of the
thoughts and intents of his heart.

HEBREWS 4:12

I pray that my husband has been born
again, not of corruptible seed but
incorruptible, through Your word, God,
which lives and abides forever.

1 PETER 1:23

———◆———

I pray that my husband never forgets that
the word of the Lord endures forever.

1 PETER 1:25

———◆———

I pray that my husband puts into practice
the fact that he shall not live by bread
alone, but by every word that proceeds
from the mouth of God.

MATTHEW 4:4

———◆———

I pray that my husband will always
understand and apply the fact that all
Scripture is given by Your inspiration, God,
and is profitable for doctrine, for
reproof, for correction, for instruction in
righteousness, that he may be

complete, thoroughly equipped for every
good work.

2 TIMOTHY 3:16–17

---◆---

I pray that my husband knows that he has
been given exceedingly great and
precious promises, that through these he
may be a partaker of the divine nature,
having escaped the corruption that is in
the world through lust.

2 PETER 1:4

---◆---

I pray that my husband always remembers
that heaven and earth will pass away,
but Jesus' words will by no means pass
away.

MATTHEW 24:35

---◆---

I pray that my husband understands the
significance of the fact that until
heaven and earth pass away, one jot or

one tittle will by no means pass from
the law till all is fulfilled.

MATTHEW 5:18

I pray that my husband takes to heart the
fact that heaven and earth will pass
away, but Your words, Jesus, will by no
means pass away.

MARK 13:31

I pray that if my husband will abide in
Your words, Jesus, he is Your disciple
indeed. And if he does that he shall know
the truth and the truth shall make him
free.

JOHN 8:31–32

I pray that my husband will remember that
Your word is a lamp to his feet and a
light to his path.

PSALM 119:105

I pray that my husband's walk with You,
Lord, will be so close that his ears shall
hear a word behind him, saying, "This is
the way, walk in it."

ISAIAH 30:21

⸻ ◆ ⸻

I pray that my husband will give attention
to Your words; O God, that he will
incline his ear to Your sayings. Do not let
them depart from his eyes and keep
them in the midst of his heart, for they are
life to him when he finds them and
health to his flesh.

PROVERBS 4:20–22

⸻ ◆ ⸻

I pray that my husband realizes the
significance of the fact that You, God,
said, "So shall My word be that goes forth
from My mouth; it shall not return to
Me void."

ISAIAH 55:11

I pray that You, O God, will instruct my husband and teach him in the way he should go and that You will guide him with Your eye.

PSALM 32:8

———————◆———————

I pray that my husband is Your servant, O God, and that You will give him understanding that he may know Your testimonies.

PSALM 119:125

———————◆———————

I pray, God, that my husband will not let Your Book of the Law depart from his mouth, but he shall meditate in it day and night, that he may observe to do according to all that is written in it. For then he will make his way prosperous, and then he will have good success.

JOSHUA 1:8

I pray, O God, that my husband will take
Your testimonies as a heritage forever,
for they are the rejoicing of his heart.

PSALM 119:111

I pray, God, that my husband will know
that every word of God is pure and
that You are a shield to those who put
their trust in You. I pray that he will not
add to Your words, lest You rebuke him,
and he be found a liar.

PROVERBS 30:5-6

23

GRIEF / HURTING

God, You know the hurt in my husband's life. And You already know other hurts that are yet to come to him. By and through Your word I pray that You will console my husband in a very special way. Wipe away his tears and bring joy back into his life. I pray Your own words for those results. Please hear and honor them in Jesus' name. Amen.

**God, in accordance
with Your Word...**

I pray that You, God, will comfort my
husband who mourns and give him
beauty for ashes, the oil of joy for
mourning, the garment of praise for
the spirit of heaviness so that he may be
called a tree of righteousness.

ISAIAH 61:2–3

I pray, O God, that You will comfort my
husband in all his tribulations, that he
may be able to comfort those who are in
any trouble, with the comfort with
which he himself is comforted by You.

2 CORINTHIANS 1:4

I pray that my husband is blessed when he
mourns for he shall be comforted.

MATTHEW 5:4

I pray that my husband will not be
ignorant concerning those who have
fallen asleep, lest he sorrow as others who
have no hope.

1 THESSALONIANS 4:13

I pray, O God, that You have comforted
my husband and will have mercy on
his affliction.

ISAIAH 49:13

I pray that when my husband passes
through the waters, You, God, will be
with him and through the rivers, they shall
not overflow him. When he walks
through the fire, he shall not be burned,
nor shall the flame scorch him.

ISAIAH 43:2

I pray that the Lord Jesus Christ Himself
and You, God, who have loved my
husband and given him everlasting
consolation and good hope by grace,
will comfort his heart and establish him in
every good word and work.

2 THESSALONIANS 2:16–17

I pray that my husband always remembers
that in You, Jesus, he does not have a
High Priest who cannot sympathize with
his weaknesses, but was in all points
tempted as he is, yet without sin. Let him
therefore come boldly to the throne of

grace, that he may obtain mercy and find grace to help in time of need.

HEBREWS 4:15–16

———◆———

I pray that though my husband may walk through the valley of the shadow of death, he will fear no evil; for You, God, are with him and Your rod and Your staff, they comfort him.

PSALM 23:4

———◆———

I pray that in this crucial time in my husband's life he can say, "O Death, where is your sting? O Hades, where is your victory?"

1 CORINTHIANS 15:55

———◆———

I pray that this is my husband's comfort in his affliction, that Your word has given him life.

PSALM 119:50

I pray that my husband will cast all his cares upon You, O God, for You care for him.

1 PETER 5:7

I pray that You, God, will wipe away every tear from my husband's eyes and that there shall be no more death, nor sorrow, nor crying. I pray that there shall be no more pain, for the former things have passed away.

REVELATION 21:4

I pray that my husband will fear not, for You, God, are with him. I pray that he will not be dismayed, for You are his God. I pray that You will strengthen him and help him and that You will uphold him with Your righteous right hand.

ISAIAH 41:10

I pray that my husband shall obtain joy
and gladness and that sorrow and
sighing shall flee away.

ISAIAH 51:11

I pray that my husband will walk by faith
and not by sight and that he is
confident, yes, well pleased rather to be
absent from the body and to be
present with You, Lord.

2 CORINTHIANS 5:7–8

24

INHERITANCE

Lord God, in Your Son's name and through Your perfect word I pray that my husband will be fully aware of and never forget the magnitude of the inheritance that awaits him. Give him a vision of that inheritance as even now I pray Your words for him. Thank You, God, in Jesus' name. Amen.

God, in accordance with Your Word...

I pray that whatever my husband does, he will do it heartily, as to You, Lord, and not to men, knowing that from You he will receive the reward of the inheritance; for he serves the Lord Christ.

COLOSSIANS 3:23–24

———◆———

I pray that my husband has been given exceedingly great and precious promises, that through these he may be a

partaker of the divine nature, having
escaped the corruption that is in the world
through lust.

2 PETER 1:4

---◆---

I pray that my husband has an inheritance
incorruptible and undefiled and that
does not fade away, reserved in heaven for
him.

1 PETER 1:4

---◆---

I commend my husband to You, God, and
to the word of Your grace, which is
able to build him up and give him an
inheritance among all those who are
sanctified.

ACTS 20:32

---◆---

I pray, God, that the Spirit Himself bears
witness with my spirit that my husband
is a child of Yours and if a child, then an

heir—an heir of Yours and a joint heir
with Christ, if indeed he suffers with Him,
that he may also be glorified together
with Him.

ROMANS 8:16–17

I pray, Lord, that my husband is aware that
eye has not seen, nor ear heard, nor
have entered into his heart the things
which You have prepared for those
who love You.

1 CORINTHIANS 2:9

I pray that my husband in You, Jesus, has
obtained an inheritance, being
predestined according to the purpose of
Him who works all things according to
the counsel of His will, that he who first
trusted in You should be to the praise
of His glory. In You, Jesus, he also trusted,
after you heard the word of truth, the
gospel of his salvation; in whom also,
having believed, he was sealed with

the Holy Spirit of promise, who is the guarantee of our inheritance until the redemption of the purchased possession, to the praise of His glory.

EPHESIANS 1:11–14

I pray that my husband always remembers that in Your house, God, are many mansions and if it were not so, Jesus would have told him. Help him to remember that Jesus has gone to prepare a place for him and if He goes and prepares a place for him, He will come again and receive him to Himself, that where He is, there he may be also.

JOHN 14:2–3

25

LONELY

Jesus, I pray to You concerning any feeling of being lonely that my husband may be experiencing now or may experience in the future. As I pray Your words, help him to remember that You said You would be with him always and that You are his constant companion. I pray Your very words to this end. In Your name I pray. Amen.

God, in accordance
with Your Word...

I pray that my husband remembers Jesus' promise to be with him always, even to the end of the age.

MATTHEW 28:20

I pray that my husband will fear not, for You, God, are with him. That he be not dismayed, for You are his God. I pray that

You will strengthen him and that You
will help him and that You will uphold him
with Your righteous right hand.

ISAIAH 41:10

---◆---

I pray that my husband's conduct will be
without covetousness, and that he will
be content with such things as he has. For
You, God, said, "I will never leave you
nor forsake you."

HEBREWS 13:5

---◆---

I pray that my husband realizes that You,
God, count the number of the stars
and call them all by name. I pray that he
remembers that great is his Lord and
mighty in power and that Your
understanding is infinite.

PSALM 147:4–5

I pray, God, that neither death nor life, nor
angels nor principalities nor powers,
nor things present nor things to come, nor
height nor depth, nor any other
created thing, shall be able to separate my
husband from Your love, God, which is
in Christ Jesus his Lord.

ROMANS 8:38–39

I pray, Jesus, that my husband remembers
Your promise that You will not leave
him as an orphan but that You will come
to him.

JOHN 14:18

I pray that my husband will be strong and
of good courage and that he does not
fear nor is he afraid, for You, the LORD his
God, are the One who goes with him. I
pray that You will not leave him nor
forsake him.

DEUTERONOMY 31:6

I pray that if my husband's father and his mother forsake him, then You, LORD, will take care of him.

PSALM 27:10

I pray that though the mountains shall depart and the hills be removed, Your kindness, God, shall not depart from my husband, nor shall Your covenant of peace be removed from him.

ISAIAH 54:10

I pray, O God, that You are my husband's refuge and strength and a very present help in trouble.

PSALM 46:1

26

LOVE

God, Your word tells us that You are love and that we must love others even as You have loved us. This is such an important matter that I want now to pray Your very words on this subject to You on my husband's behalf. Honor Your words Lord as my prayers for my husband. Thank You for the privilege of praying in Jesus' name. Amen.

God, in accordance with Your Word...

I pray that my husband will love others, for love is of You, God.

1 JOHN 4:7

I pray that my husband understands the true meaning of love and that though he speaks with the tongues of men and of angels, but has not love, he has

become sounding brass or a clanging
cymbal. And though he has the gift of
prophecy, and understands all mysteries
and all knowledge, and though he has
all faith, so that he can remove mountains,
but has not love, he is nothing. And
though he bestows all his goods to feed
the poor, and though he gives his body
to be burned, but has not love, it profits
him nothing. I pray that he remembers
that love suffers long and is kind; love
does not envy; love does not parade
itself, is not puffed up; does not behave
rudely, does not seek its own, is not
provoked, thinks no evil; does not rejoice
in iniquity, but rejoices in the truth;
bears all things, believes all things, hopes
all things, endures all things. Help him
to understand that love never fails. Help
him to abide in faith, hope, love, these
three; but the greatest of these is love.

1 CORINTHIANS 13:1–8, 13

I pray that my husband understands that
love is not that he loved You, God, but

that You loved him and sent Your Son to
be the propitiation for his sins. And
help him to know that if You so loved him,
he also ought to love others.

1 JOHN 4:10–11

---◆---

I pray that my husband totally understands
that as You, God, loved Jesus, He also
loves him and he is to abide in His love.

JOHN 15:9

---◆---

I pray that if my husband has Jesus'
commandments and keeps them, it is
he who loves Him. And my husband who
loves Jesus will be loved by You, God,
and Jesus will love him and manifest
Himself to him.

JOHN 14:21

---◆---

I pray that You, God, will bring to my
husband's mind that it is Jesus'

commandment that he love others just as
He has loved him.

JOHN 15:12

———— ◆ ————

I pray that my husband shall love You, the
Lord his God, with all his heart, with
all his soul, with all his mind, and with all
his strength and that he shall love his
neighbor as himself.

MARK 12:30–31

———— ◆ ————

I pray that my husband has known and
believed the love that You, God, have
for him and that he who loves You must
love his brother also.

1 JOHN 4:16, 21

———— ◆ ————

I pray, God, that You have loved my
husband with an everlasting love and

with lovingkindness have drawn him to
You.

JOHN 16:27

———————◆———————

I pray that You, God, love my husband,
because he has loved Jesus, and has
believed that He came forth from You.

JOHN 16:27

———————◆———————

I pray that my husband will realize that
You, God, demonstrated Your own love
toward him in that while he was still a
sinner, Christ died for him.

ROMANS 5:8

———————◆———————

I pray that You, God, so loved my husband
that You gave Your only begotten Son,
that he who believes in Him should not
perish but have everlasting life.

JOHN 3:16

I pray that neither death nor life, nor
angels nor principalities nor powers,
nor things present nor things to come, nor
height nor depth, nor any other
created thing, shall be able to separate my
husband from Your love, God, which is
in Christ Jesus his Lord.

ROMANS 8:38–39

I pray, Jesus, that my husband will take
heed to the new commandment You
gave to him that he love others as You
have loved him and that by this he will
know that he is Your disciple, if he has
love for others.

JOHN 13:34–35

27
LOVE FOR MY HUSBAND

Lord, I pray these, Your words for my husband. Honor my prayers by honoring Your own words. I praise You and pray to You in Jesus' name. Amen.

God, in accordance
with Your Word...

I pray that while my husband and I have not seen You, God, at any time, if we love one another, You abide in us, and Your love has been perfected in us.

1 JOHN 4:12

I pray, Jesus, that my husband and I will follow Your commandment that we love one another as You have loved us.

JOHN 15:12

I pray that if You, God, so loved my husband and me, we also ought to love one another.

1 JOHN 4:11

I pray, Lord Jesus, that by this my husband and I know love, because You laid down Your life for us. And we also ought to lay down our lives for each other.

1 JOHN 3:16

I pray, Jesus, that my husband and I will follow Your command that we love one another.

JOHN 15:17

I pray that my husband and I may with one mind and one mouth glorify the God and Father of our Lord Jesus Christ.

ROMANS 15:6

I pray, Lord God, that my husband and I
will love one another, for love is of
You; and everyone who loves is born of
You and knows You. But if we do not
love we do not know You, for You are love.

1 JOHN 4:7–8

I pray that my husband and I will always
understand the significance of the
question, "Can two walk together, unless
they are agreed?"

AMOS 3:3

28

MARITAL PROBLEMS

Lord God, I pray as my prayers today Your perfect word. I ask You to honor Your word in this very sensitive area and to be with my husband in every way possible. I love You and I love my husband. Be with him now. In Jesus' name I ask You to bless the praying of Your word at all times. Thank You for hearing my prayers. Amen.

God, in accordance
with Your Word...

I pray that as for my husband and my house, we will serve You, LORD.

JOSHUA 24:15

I pray that my husband has read that You, the LORD God, said, "It is not good that man should be alone; I will make him a helper comparable to him."

GENESIS 2:18

I pray that my husband always
understands that a man shall leave his
father and mother and be joined to his
wife, and they shall become one flesh.

GENESIS 2:24

I pray that my husband will behave wisely
in a perfect way and that we will walk
within our house with a perfect heart.

PSALM 101:2

I pray that my husband and I will be of
one mind, having compassion for one
another, that we will be tenderhearted and
courteous, not returning evil for evil or
reviling for reviling, but on the contrary
blessing, knowing that we were called
to this, that we may inherit a blessing.

1 PETER 3:8–9

I pray, God, that my husband and I will let all bitterness, wrath, anger, clamor, and evil speaking be put away from us, with all malice. And that we will be kind to one another, tenderhearted, forgiving one another, just as You, God, in Christ forgave us.

EPHESIANS 4:31–32

I pray that my husband and I will trust in You, LORD, with all our hearts and lean not on our own understanding and that in all our ways we will acknowledge You, O God, and that You shall direct our paths.

PROVERBS 3:5–6

I pray that my husband and I remember that hatred stirs up strife but love covers all sins.

PROVERBS 10:12

I pray that since my husband and I have purified our souls in obeying the truth through the Spirit in sincere love of each other, that we will love one another fervently with a pure heart.

1 PETER 1:22

29

MARRIAGE

Holy Father, You have given us marriage as something sacred. It is important to You and it is important to us. Hear now Your words as my prayers and honor them according to Your promises. I pray in Jesus' name, and I thank You in His will. Amen.

God, in accordance
with Your Word...

I pray that I will not depart from my husband.

1 CORINTHIANS 7:10

I pray that I will love my husband.

TITUS 2:4

I pray that as the elect of God, holy and beloved, that my husband and I put on tender mercies, kindness, humility,

meekness, and longsuffering. I pray
that we will bear with one another,
forgiving one another, if we have a
complaint against each other, even as
Christ forgave us, so we also must do.
But above all these things help us to put
on love, which is the bond of
perfection.

COLOSSIANS 3:12–14

30

NEEDS

Lord, You and You alone know all of my husband's needs. I desire now to spend time with You praying Your word over his needs and to ask You to bless the praying of Your word and to honor the praying of Your word by meeting my husband's needs as only You can do. I pray Your words now in Jesus' name. Amen.

God, in accordance with Your Word...

I pray that my husband will delight himself also in You, LORD, and that You will give him the desires of his heart.

PSALM 37:4

I pray that You, God, will open Your hand and satisfy the desire of my husband.

PSALM 145:16

I pray that You, Lord, will guide my
husband continually.

ISAIAH 58:11

---◆---

I pray that my husband will not spend
wages for what does not satisfy and
that he will listen carefully to You, God,
and will let his soul delight itself in
abundance.

ISAIAH 55:2

---◆---

I pray that whatever things my husband
asks for in prayer, believing, he will
receive.

MATTHEW 21:22

---◆---

I pray, Jesus, that if my husband asks
anything in Your name You will do it.

JOHN 14:14

I pray, Lord Jesus, that if my husband abides in You and Your words abide in him, he will ask what he desires, and it shall be done for him.

JOHN 15:7

I pray that my husband will ask in Your name, Jesus, and he will receive, that his joy may be full.

JOHN 16:24

I pray that my husband shall know the truth and the truth shall make him free.

JOHN 8:32

I pray that You, the God and Father of our Lord Jesus Christ, have blessed my husband with every spiritual blessing in the heavenly places in Christ.

EPHESIANS 1:3

I pray that my husband can do all things
through Christ who strengthens him.

PHILIPPIANS 4:13

◆

I pray that You, my God, shall supply all
my husband's needs according to Your
riches in glory by Christ Jesus.

PHILIPPIANS 4:19

◆

I pray that if my husband's heart does not
condemn him, he has confidence
toward You, God, and whatever he asks he
receives from You, because he keeps
Your commandments and does those
things that are pleasing in Your sight.

1 JOHN 3:21–22

31

OBEDIENCE

God, You have said that obedience is more important to You than is sacrifice. Because I believe that You meant what You said I now pray back to You Your powerful words. God, in Jesus' name, I ask You to help my husband be obedient to You in every way and in every situation. Having asked You for it in Jesus' name, I believe that it will happen and I thank You in His name. Amen.

God, in accordance
with Your Word...

I pray that my husband recognizes the fact
that You, God, have set before him
today a blessing and a curse: the blessing,
if he obeys the commandments of the
LORD his God, which You have commanded
him today; and the curse, if he does
not obey the commandments of the LORD
his God, but turns aside from the way

which You command him today, to go
after other gods he has not known.

DEUTERONOMY 11:26–28

I pray that my husband never forgets that
to obey is better than sacrifice.

1 SAMUEL 15:22

I pray that my husband will heed Your
commandments, O God, so that his
peace will be like a river and his
righteousness like the waves of the sea.

ISAIAH 48:18

I pray, O God, that my husband will obey
Your voice, and You will be his God,
and he shall be Your child. And that he will
walk in all the ways that You have
commanded him, that it may be well with
him.

JEREMIAH 7:23

I pray, Lord Jesus, that my husband loves
You and keeps Your commandments.

JOHN 14:15

I pray, God, that my husband knows that
he ought to obey You rather than men.

ACTS 5:29

I pray, Jesus, that my husband will always
keep Your commandments.

1 JOHN 2:3

I pray that my husband will learn Your
statutes, O God, and be careful to
observe them. I pray that he will be careful
to do as You, the LORD his God, have
commanded him and that he shall not
turn aside to the right hand or to the
left. I pray that he will walk in all the ways

which You have commanded him, and
that you may prolong his days.

DEUTERONOMY 5:1, 32–33

I pray that my husband will walk in Your
ways, God, to keep Your statutes and
Your commandments, and that You will
lengthen his days.

1 KINGS 3:14

I pray that You, God, will teach my
husband to do Your will, for You are
his God.

PSALM 143:10

I pray that whatever my husband does, he
does it heartily, as to the Lord and not
to men.

COLOSSIANS 3:23

32

PATIENCE

Lord Jesus, patience is so important but so elusive. I pray to You now what You have already declared in Your word, and I ask You to honor it in my husband's life. Bless now the praying of Your word. Amen.

God, in accordance with Your Word...

I pray that whatever things were written before were written for my husband's learning, that he through the patience and comfort of the Scriptures might have hope. Now may You, the God of patience and comfort, grant my husband to be like-minded toward others, according to Christ Jesus.

ROMANS 15:4–5

I pray that my husband will glory in
tribulations, knowing that tribulation
produces perseverance; and perseverance,
character; and character, hope.

ROMANS 5:3–4

I pray that my husband will rest in You,
LORD, and that he will wait patiently for
You. I pray that he does not fret because of
him who prospers in his way or
because of the man who brings wicked
schemes to pass. I pray that he will
cease from anger, and forsake wrath and
that he does not fret—it only causes
harm.

PSALM 37:7–8

I pray that my husband will wait patiently
for You, LORD, and that You will incline
Yourself to him and hear his cry.

PSALM 40:1

I pray that my husband will imitate those
who through faith and patience inherit
the promises.

HEBREWS 6:12

◆

I pray that my husband does not cast away
his confidence, which has great reward.
For he has need of endurance, so that after
he has done Your will, God, he may
receive the promise.

HEBREWS 10:35-36

◆

I pray that my husband will not hasten in
his spirit to be angry, for anger rests in
the bosom of fools.

ECCLESIASTES 7:9

◆

I pray that since my husband is
surrounded by so great a cloud of
witnesses, let him lay aside every weight,
and the sin which so easily ensnares

him, and let him run with endurance the race that is set before him.

HEBREWS 12:1

---◆---

I pray that the fruit of the Spirit in my husband is love, joy, peace, longsuffering, kindness, goodness, faithfulness, gentleness, and self-control.

GALATIANS 5:22–23

---◆---

I pray that my husband will wait on You, Lord, and that he shall renew his strength. I pray that he shall mount up with wings like eagles and that he shall run and not be weary and walk and not faint.

ISAIAH 40:31

---◆---

I pray that my husband will wait on You, Lord, and that he will be of good courage. I also pray that You will

strengthen his heart and that he will
wait on You.

PSALM 27:14

———◆———

I pray that my husband will hope and wait
quietly for Your salvation, O LORD.

LAMENTATIONS 3:26

———◆———

I pray that my husband will hope for what
he does not see and eagerly wait for it
with perseverance.

ROMANS 8:25

———◆———

I pray that my husband understands that
the testing of his faith produces
patience and that he should let patience
have its perfect work, that he may be
perfect and complete, lacking nothing.

JAMES 1:3–4

I pray that my husband will be patient
until Your coming, Lord. I pray that he
will see how the farmer waits for the
precious fruit of the earth, waiting
patiently for it until it receives the early
and latter rain and that he also will be
patient, for Your coming is at hand.

JAMES 5:7 8

33

PEACE

Heavenly Father, just as Your word says, I pray perfect peace for my husband. There is no process more important to his having peace than to pray Your words of promise. I pray Your words in Jesus' name, and I thank You for hearing and answering. Amen.

God, in accordance
with Your Word...

I pray, God, that You will keep my husband
in perfect peace, whose mind is stayed
on You, because he trusts in You.

ISAIAH 26:3

I pray that Your kindness, God, shall not
depart from my husband, nor shall
Your covenant of peace be removed from
him.

ISAIAH 54:10

I pray that my husband will lie down in
peace, and sleep; for You alone,
O Lord, make him dwell in safety.

PSALM 4:8

———————◆———————

I pray, O Lord, that You will give strength
to my husband and that You will bless
him with peace.

PSALM 29:11

———————◆———————

I pray that You, Jesus, have left Your peace
with my husband. I pray that his heart
will not be troubled, neither will he be
afraid.

JOHN 14:27

———————◆———————

I pray that my husband who has been
justified by faith, will have peace with
You, God, through his Lord Jesus Christ.

ROMANS 5:1

I pray that Jesus Himself is my husband's peace.

EPHESIANS 2:14

I pray that my husband will be anxious for nothing, but in everything by prayer and supplication, with thanksgiving, will let his requests be made known to You, God; and Your peace which surpasses all understanding, will guard his heart and mind through Christ Jesus.

PHILIPPIANS 4:6-7

34
POWER

Lord God, my husband is in need of Your power. That power comes only through Your word, and that is what I pray to You today. Honor the praying of Your word and bring Your power into the life of my husband. It is in the powerful name of Jesus that I offer up Your words in prayer for my husband. Thank You for hearing and answering each of these prayers. Amen.

**God, in accordance
with Your Word...**

I pray that my husband will take pleasure
in infirmities, in reproaches, in needs,
in persecutions, in distresses, for Christ's
sake. For when he is weak, then he is
strong.

2 CORINTHIANS 12:10

I pray that in all things my husband is
more than a conqueror through Jesus
who loved him.

ROMANS 8:37

I pray that my husband can do all things
through Christ who strengthens him.

PHILIPPIANS 4:13

I pray, Jesus, that whatever my husband
asks in Your name that You will do,
that the Father may be glorified in the Son.

JOHN 14:13

I pray that You, God, are able to make all
grace abound toward my husband,
that he, always having all sufficiency in all
things, may have an abundance for
every good work.

2 CORINTHIANS 9:8

I pray, Jesus, that Your grace is sufficient
for my husband, for Your strength is
made perfect in weakness.

2 CORINTHIANS 12:9

I pray that my husband will see the
exceeding greatness of Your power,
God, toward he who believes, according to
the working of Your mighty power.

EPHESIANS 1:19

I pray, O God, that You are able to do
exceedingly abundantly above all that
my husband asks or thinks, according to
the power that works in him.

EPHESIANS 3:20

35

PRAISE

Heavenly Father, we were created to praise You. Through the praying of Your word I petition You to put into my husband's heart a consistent desire to praise You at all times. These words of Yours are my prayers in Jesus' name. Amen.

God, in accordance with Your Word...

I pray, LORD God, that my husband will sing praises to You and that he will declare Your deeds among the people.

PSALM 9:11

I pray that my husband will sing to You, LORD, as long as he lives.

PSALM 104:33

I pray that every day my husband will bless You, God, and will praise Your name forever and ever.

PSALM 145:2

———◆———

I pray that my husband will know that great is the LORD, and greatly to be praised and that Your greatness is unsearchable.

PSALM 145:3

———◆———

I pray that my husband's tongue shall speak of Your righteousness, LORD, and of Your praise all the day long.

PSALM 35:28

———◆———

I pray, O LORD, that You will open my husband's lips and his mouth shall show forth Your praise.

PSALM 51:15

I pray, O LORD, that my husband will praise
You.

ISAIAH 12:1

---◆---

I pray that my husband will give You
thanks, O Lord God Almighty, the One
who is and who was and who is to come,
because You have taken Your great
power and reigned.

REVELATION 11:17

---◆---

I pray that my husband will hope
continually, O God, and will praise You
yet more and more.

PSALM 71:14

---◆---

I pray, God, that my husband will enter
into Your gates with thanksgiving, and
into Your courts with praise.

PSALM 100:4

I pray that You, LORD, are my husband's
strength and song, and that You have
become his salvation; that You are his
God, and that he will praise You.

EXODUS 15:2

———◆———

I pray that my husband will proclaim the
name of the LORD and ascribe greatness
to You his God.

DEUTERONOMY 32:3

———◆———

I pray that my husband will proclaim, "The
LORD lives! Blessed be my Rock! Let
God be exalted, the Rock of my salvation!"

2 SAMUEL 22:47

———◆———

I pray that my husband always remembers
that You, LORD, are great and greatly to
be praised.

1 CHRONICLES 16:25

I pray that my husband will bless You, LORD, at all times and that Your praise shall continually be in his mouth.

PSALM 34:1

I pray, God, that You have put a new song in my husband's mouth—praise to his God.

PSALM 40:3

I pray that my husband realizes that great is the LORD, and greatly to be praised.

PSALM 48:1

I pray that my husband prays, "Blessed be the LORD, who daily loads me with benefits."

PSALM 68:19

I pray that my husband will give thanks to You, LORD, for You are good! For Your mercy endures forever.

PSALM 106:1

◆

I pray that You will let my husband's soul live, O God, and it shall praise You.

PSALM 119:175

◆

I pray that my husband will praise You, God, for he is fearfully and wonderfully made. Marvelous are Your works, and that his soul knows very well.

PSALM 139:14

◆

I pray that my husband's mouth shall speak the praise of You, LORD.

PSALM 145:21

I pray that my husband will praise You, LORD!

PSALM 146:1

◆

I pray that my husband will praise You, God, for Your mighty acts and that he will praise You according to Your excellent greatness!

PSALM 150:2

◆

I pray that my husband will continually offer the sacrifice of praise to You, God, that is, the fruit of his lips, giving thanks to Your name.

HEBREWS 13:15

36

PROTECTION

Lord God, honor the prayers I lift up to You for my husband's protection. They are Your words straight from Your Bible. Protect him at all times through the praying of Your word in Jesus' name. Amen.

God, in accordance
with Your Word...

I pray that my husband's LORD God, who goes before him, will fight for him.

DEUTERONOMY 1:30

I pray that if my husband will indeed obey Your voice, God, and do all that You speak, then You will be an enemy to his enemies and an adversary to his adversaries.

EXODUS 23:22

I pray that no weapon formed against my husband shall prosper and every tongue which rises against him in judgment You, God, shall condemn.

ISAIAH 54:17

I pray that Jesus has given my husband the authority to trample on serpents and scorpions, and over all the power of the enemy, and nothing shall by any means hurt him.

LUKE 10:19

I pray that You, Lord, are faithful, who will establish my husband and guard him from the evil one.

2 THESSALONIANS 3:3

I pray that if God be for my husband, who can be against him?

ROMANS 8:31

37

REBELLIOUS

Lord God, through the power of Your word I pray that no spirit of rebellion will ever enter into my husband. Through the praying of Your word keep him free from any rebellious spirit or attitude. I pray to You and I thank You in Jesus' precious name. Amen.

God, in accordance
with Your Word...

I pray that my husband, by doing good, may put to silence the ignorance of foolish men.

1 PETER 2:15

———◆———

I pray that if my husband is willing and obedient he shall eat the good of the land.

ISAIAH 1:19

I pray that my husband will gird up the
loins of his mind, be sober, and rest his
hope fully upon the grace that is to be
brought to him at the revelation of Jesus
Christ; as an obedient child, not conforming
himself to the former lusts, as in his
ignorance; but as You, God, who called
him is holy, he also is to be holy in all
his conduct.

1 PETER 1:13–15

I pray that my husband is aware that
rebellion is as the sin of witchcraft.

1 SAMUEL 15:23

I pray, God, that my husband knows that
You resist the proud, but give grace to
the humble and that he will humble
himself under Your mighty hand, that
You, God, may exalt him in due time.

1 PETER 5:5–6

I pray that my husband will obey those who rule over him, and be submissive, for they watch out for his soul, as those who must give account.

HEBREWS 13:17

I pray that my husband will be like Jesus and humble himself and become obedient.

PHILIPPIANS 2:8

I pray that like You, Jesus, my husband learns obedience by the things he suffers.

HEBREWS 5:8

I pray that my husband knows and understands that no grave trouble will overtake the righteous, but the wicked shall be filled with evil.

PROVERBS 12:21

I pray that my husband will submit to You,
God. That he will resist the devil and
he will flee from him.

JAMES 4:7

I pray that while my husband was once
darkness, now he is light in the Lord
and that he will walk as a child of light.

EPHESIANS 5:8

I pray that my husband will no longer walk
in the futility of his mind.

EPHESIANS 4:17

I pray that my husband does not let sin
reign in his mortal body, that he should
obey it in its lusts. I also pray that he does
not present his members as instruments
of unrighteousness to sin, but that he
presents himself to You, God, as being

alive from the dead, and his members as
instruments of righteousness to God.
For sin shall not have dominion over him,
for he is not under law but under grace.

ROMANS 6:12–14

38

SALVATION

Lord, the most important thing in life is salvation. I pray for my husband's salvation through the powerful praying of Your Holy Word. Hear these my prayers for my husband. Honor them. And bless him with Your salvation. In Jesus' name I pray. Amen.

God, in accordance
with Your Word...

I pray that my husband will discover that Jesus said, "He who believes in Me has everlasting life."

JOHN 6:47

I pray that my husband remembers that Jesus has come to seek and to save that which was lost.

LUKE 19:19

I pray, Lord Jesus, that my husband will come to understand what You meant when You said, "Therefore whoever confesses Me before men, him I will also confess before My Father who is in heaven."

MATTHEW 10:32

———————◆———————

I pray that if my husband will confess with his mouth the Lord Jesus and believe in his heart that God has raised Him from the dead, he will be saved. For with his heart he believes unto righteousness, and with his mouth confession is made unto salvation.

ROMANS 10:9–10

———————◆———————

I pray that You, God, so loved my husband that You gave Your only begotten Son, that if my husband believes in Him he should not perish but have everlasting life.

JOHN 3:16

I pray, God, that You did not send Your Son
into the world to condemn my husband,
but that my husband through Him might
be saved.

JOHN 3:17

———————◆———————

I pray that this will be my husband's
testimony: that You, God, have given
him eternal life, and this life is in Your
Son.

1 JOHN 5:11

———————◆———————

I pray that by grace my husband has been
saved through faith, and that not of
himself; it is the gift of God, not of works,
lest he should boast.

EPHESIANS 2:8–9

———————◆———————

I pray that You, God, have saved my
husband and called him with a holy
calling, not according to his works, but

according to Your own purpose and
grace which was given to him in Christ
Jesus before time began.

2 TIMOTHY 1:9

———————◆———————

I pray, God, that it is not by works of
righteousness which my husband has
done, but according to Your mercy You
saved him, through the washing of
regeneration and renewing of the Holy
Spirit, whom You poured out on him
abundantly through Jesus Christ his Savior.

TITUS 3:5–6

———————◆———————

I pray, God, that Jesus stands at the door
and knocks and if my husband hears
His voice and opens the door, He will come
in to him and dine with him, and him
with Him.

REVELATION 3:20

I pray, God, that my husband has been born again, not of corruptible seed but incorruptible, through Your word which lives and abides forever.

1 PETER 1:23

39

SATAN DEFEATED

Heavenly Father, my husband's enemy is Satan. He wants to destroy him. But God, Your word is stronger than even Satan and that is what I pray on my husband's behalf. God, please honor the praying of Your word and defeat Satan in his life. Thank You, God, in the powerful name of Jesus. Amen.

God, in accordance
with Your Word...

I pray that my husband will be strong in You, Lord, and in the power of Your might. I pray that he will put on the whole armor of God, that he may be able to stand against the wiles of the devil. For he does not wrestle against flesh and blood, but against principalities, against powers, against the rulers of the darkness of this age, against spiritual hosts of

wickedness in the heavenly places. I
pray that he will take up Your whole armor,
God, that he may be able to withstand
in the evil day, and having done all, to
stand. I pray that he has girded his waist
with truth, having put on the breastplate of
righteousness, and having shod his feet
with the preparation of the gospel of peace,
and above all, taking the shield of faith
with which he will be able to quench all
the fiery darts of the wicked one. I pray
that he also takes the helmet of salvation,
and the sword of the Spirit, which is
the word of God; praying always with all
prayer and supplication in the Spirit,
being watchful to this end with all
perseverance and supplication for all
the saints.

EPHESIANS 6:10–18

I pray that You, God, will open my husband's
eyes, in order to turn them from
darkness to light, and from the power of
Satan to God, that he may receive
forgiveness of sins and an inheritance

among those who are sanctified by faith
in Jesus.

ACTS 26:18

---◆---

I pray, God, that You preserve the soul of
my husband and deliver him out of the
hand of the wicked.

PSALM 97:10

---◆---

I pray, God, for my husband that the Son
of God was manifested, that He might
destroy the works of the devil.

1 JOHN 3:8

---◆---

I pray for my husband that he puts off,
concerning his former conduct, the
old man which grows corrupt according to
the deceitful lusts, and be renewed in
the spirit of his mind, and that he put
on the new man which was created

according to You, God, in true righteousness and holiness.

EPHESIANS 4:22–24

———————◆———————

I pray, Jesus, that my husband knows that You have disarmed principalities and powers, and have made a public spectacle of them, triumphing over them in it.

COLOSSIANS 2:15

———————◆———————

I pray that my husband is strong, and that the word of God abides in him and he has overcome the wicked one.

1 JOHN 2:14

———————◆———————

I pray, God, that my husband understands that even the angels who did not keep their proper domain, but left their own abode, You have reserved in everlasting

chains under darkness for the judgment of
the great day.

JUDE 1:6

———◆———

I pray that my husband will not give place
to the devil.

EPHESIANS 4:27

———◆———

I do not pray, God, that You should take
my husband out of the world, but that
You should keep him from the evil one.

JOHN 17:15

———◆———

I pray that my husband will submit to You,
God, and that he will resist the devil
and he will flee from him.

JAMES 4:7

———◆———

I pray that my husband will be sober and
vigilant, because his adversary the devil

walks about like a roaring lion, seeking whom he may devour. I pray that he will resist him, steadfast in the faith, knowing that the same sufferings are experienced by other Christians in the world.

1 PETER 5:8–9

I pray that at this time my husband will remember that Jesus went about doing good and healing all who were oppressed by the devil, for God was with Him.

ACTS 10:38

I pray that You, God, have delivered my husband from the power of darkness and conveyed him into the kingdom of Jesus, in whom he has redemption through His blood, the forgiveness of sins.

COLOSSIANS 1:13–14

I pray that in all things my husband is more than a conqueror through Him who loved him.

ROMANS 8:37

———◆———

I pray, God, that the accuser of my husband, who accuses him before his God day and night, has been cast down. I pray that he overcame him by the blood of the Lamb and by the word of his testimony.

REVELATION 12:10–11

———◆———

I pray that neither death nor life, nor angels nor principalities nor powers, nor things present nor things to come, nor height nor depth, nor any other created thing, shall be able to separate my husband from the love of God which is in Christ Jesus his Lord.

ROMANS 8:38–39

I pray that while my husband is hard pressed on every side, yet not crushed; he is perplexed, but not in despair; persecuted, but not forsaken; struck down, but not destroyed—always carrying about in his body the dying of the Lord Jesus, that the life of Jesus also may be manifested in his body.

2 CORINTHIANS 4:8–10

———◆———

I pray that my husband has his senses exercised to discern both good and evil.

HEBREWS 5:14

———◆———

I pray that though my husband walks in the flesh, he does not war according to the flesh. For the weapons of his warfare are not carnal but mighty in God for pulling down strongholds, casting down arguments and every high thing that exalts itself against the knowledge of God,

bringing every thought into captivity
to the obedience of Christ.

2 CORINTHIANS 10:3–5

———◆———

I pray, God, that Your presence will go with
my husband forever.

EXODUS 33:14

———◆———

I pray, God, that my husband will be strong
and of good courage; that he is not
afraid, nor dismayed, for You, the LORD his
God, are with him wherever he goes.

JOSHUA 1:9

———◆———

I pray, God, that You will preserve the soul
of my husband and that You will deliver
him out of the hand of the wicked.

PSALM 97:10

I pray, Lord, that You will guard my husband
from the evil one.

2 THESSALONIANS 3:3

I pray, God, that You are my husband's
refuge and that You will thrust out the
enemy from before him.

DEUTERONOMY 33:27

I pray, God, that the angel of the LORD
encamps all around my husband who
fears You, and delivers him.

PSALM 34:7

I pray that Satan will not take advantage of
my husband for he is not ignorant of
his devices.

2 CORINTHIANS 2:11

I pray that my husband know that he does
not live by bread alone, but by every
word that proceeds from the mouth of You,
God.

MATTHEW 4:4

I pray, Lord, that my husband will drive
Satan away by worshipping the Lord
his God, and Him only he shall serve.

MATTHEW 4:10

I pray that my husband will gird up the
loins of his mind and be sober, and
rest his hope fully upon the grace that is to
be brought to him at the revelation of
Jesus Christ; as an obedient child, not
conforming himself to the former lusts,
as in his ignorance; but as You, God, who
called him is holy, may he also be holy
in all his conduct.

1 PETER 1:13–15

I pray that my husband will have the mind
of Christ.

1 CORINTHIANS 2:16

40

SECURITY

Lord, real and true security comes only from You. I pray Your words concerning security for my husband. Through the praying of Your word help him to sense the security that only You can give. Lord, I thank You and I pray in Your name. Amen.

God, in accordance with Your Word...

I pray that my husband is persuaded that neither death nor life, nor angels nor principalities nor powers, nor things present nor things to come, nor height nor depth, nor any other created thing, shall be able to separate him from the love of God which is in Christ Jesus his Lord.

ROMANS 8:38–39

I pray that in Jesus my husband also trusted, after he heard the word of truth, the

gospel of his salvation; in whom also,
having believed, he was sealed with
the Holy Spirit of promise.

EPHESIANS 1:13

I pray that surely goodness and mercy shall
follow my husband all the days of his
life and that he will dwell in the house of
the LORD forever.

PSALM 23:6

I pray that my husband is one of those
who has come to You, Jesus, and who
You will by no means cast out.

JOHN 6:37

I pray, Jesus, that my husband has heard
Your voice and that You know him, and
that he follows You, and that You will give

him eternal life, and he shall never
perish.

JOHN 10:27–28

———◆———

I pray that my husband does not grieve
the Holy Spirit of God, by whom he
was sealed for the day of redemption.

EPHESIANS 4:30

———◆———

I pray that You, God, who have begun a
good work in my husband will complete
it until the day of Jesus Christ.

PHILIPPIANS 1:6

———◆———

I pray, Lord, that Your faithfulness will
establish my husband and guard him
from the evil one.

2 THESSALONIANS 3:3

I pray that You, God, are able to keep my
husband from stumbling, and to
present him faultless before the presence
of Your glory with exceeding joy.

JUDE 1:24

41

SERVING GOD

Lord God, in accordance with Your perfect word I pray that my husband will walk after You and that he will serve You. Your word is clear that he cannot serve two masters. Now—at this very moment—I ask You to honor Your word in the area of my husband's service to You. Use Your Holy Spirit to guide him and direct him in this area of his life in accordance with Your word which I now pray. Thank You in Jesus' name. Amen.

God, in accordance with Your Word...

I pray that my husband will walk after You, the LORD his God, and fear You, and keep Your commandments and obey Your voice, and that he shall serve You and hold fast to You.

DEUTERONOMY 13:4

I pray, God, that my husband knows that he cannot serve two masters; for either he will hate the one and love the other, or else he will be loyal to the one and despise the other. He cannot serve You and mammon.

MATTHEW 6:24

I pray to You, God, that my husband will present his body a living sacrifice, holy, acceptable to You, which is his reasonable service. I pray also that he will not be conformed to this world, but be transformed by the renewing of his mind, that he may prove what is that good and acceptable and perfect will of Yours, God.

ROMANS 12:1–2

I pray that my husband will serve You, the LORD his God, and You only he shall serve.

MATTHEW 4:10

I pray that my husband will love you, the LORD his God, and walk in all Your ways, keeping Your commandments, and holding fast to You, and will serve You with all his heart and with all his soul.

JOSHUA 22:5

I pray that my husband will be kindly affectionate to others with brotherly love, in honor giving preference to others; not lagging in diligence, fervent in spirit, serving You, Lord; rejoicing in hope, patient in tribulation, continuing steadfastly in prayer; distributing to the needs of the saints, given to hospitality.

ROMANS 12:10–13

I pray, O God, that my husband shall serve You, the LORD his God.

EXODUS 23:25

I pray that my husband will fear You, the
LORD his God, and walk in all Your ways
and love You, and serve You, the LORD his
God, with all his heart and with all his
soul and that he will keep Your
commandments and Your statutes
which You command him today for his
good.

DEUTERONOMY 10:12–13

---◆---

I pray that my husband does not turn aside
from following You, LORD, but serves
You with all his heart. I pray that he does
not turn aside, for then he would go
after empty things which cannot profit or
deliver, for they are nothing. For You
will not forsake him, for Your great name's
sake, because it has pleased You to
make him Yours.

1 SAMUEL 12:20–22

---◆---

I pray that my husband will know You,
God, and serve You with a loyal heart

and with a willing mind; for You search all
hearts and understand all the intent of
the thoughts. If he seeks You, You will be
found by him; but if he forsakes You,
You will cast him off forever.

1 CHRONICLES 28:9

◆

I pray that my husband has been delivered
from the law, having died to what he
was held by, so that he should serve in the
newness of the Spirit and not in the
oldness of the letter.

ROMANS 7:6

◆

I pray that my husband will serve You, LORD,
with gladness and come before Your
presence with singing. I pray that he will
know that You, LORD, are God and that
it is You who has made him, and not he
himself.

PSALM 100:2–3

42

SICKNESS

Heavenly Father, in accordance with the perfection of Your word I pray that You will heal my husband of his affliction and restore his health. We need Your help and pray Your word for that important need to be met. It is in the powerful name of Jesus that I pray these prayers to You. Amen.

God, in accordance with Your Word...

I pray that You will heal my husband, O LORD, and he shall be healed. Save him and he shall be saved.

JEREMIAH 17:14

I pray, God, that You will restore health to my husband and heal his wounds.

JEREMIAH 30:17

I pray that my husband will diligently heed Your voice, LORD God, and do what is right in Your sight and give ear to Your commandments and keep all Your statutes, and that You will put no diseases on him.

EXODUS 15:26

I pray, O God, that Jesus was wounded for my husband's transgressions and was bruised for his iniquities and by His stripes he is healed.

ISAIAH 53:5

I pray, God, that You heal all my husband's diseases and redeem his life from destruction.

PSALM 103:3–4

I pray that Jesus Himself bore my husband's sins in His own body on the tree, and

that he, having died to sin, might live for
righteousness—by whose stripes he
was healed.

1 PETER 2:24

◆

I pray that my husband may prosper in all
things and be in health, just as his soul
prospers.

3 JOHN 1:2

◆

I pray, O God, that my husband remembers
that Jesus healed every sickness and
every disease among the people.

MATTHEW 9:35

◆

I pray, Jesus, that power goes out from You
and heals my husband.

LUKE 6:19

I pray, God, that You have sent Your word
and healed my husband and delivered
him from destruction.

PSALM 107:20

---◆---

I pray, God, that I am not worthy that You
should come under my roof. But only
speak a word, and my husband will be
healed.

MATTHEW 8:8

---◆---

I pray that the prayer of faith will save my
husband from his sickness and that You,
Lord, will raise him up. And if he has
committed sins, he will be forgiven.

JAMES 5:15

43

SPIRITUAL GROWTH

Lord Jesus, there is no more powerful prayer that I can pray than to pray the word of God directly from the pages of the Bible. That is what I now do as I pray for my husband's spiritual growth. I pray that as Your word says he will take heed to himself and keep himself in accordance with Your word. Thank You for honoring Your words that I pray to You now. Amen.

God, in accordance
with Your Word...

I pray that my husband will beware, lest there be in him an evil heart of unbelief in departing from the living God. I pray that I will exhort him daily, while it is called "Today," lest he be hardened through the deceitfulness of sin.

HEBREWS 3:12–13

I pray that my husband does not forget
You, the LORD his God, by not keeping
Your commandments, Your judgments,
and Your statutes which You command
him today. I pray that he shall remember
the LORD his God, for it is You who
gives him power to get wealth.

DEUTERONOMY 8:11, 18

I pray that my husband has not forgotten
the name of his God, or stretched out
his hands to a foreign god. Would You,
God, not search this out? For You know
the secrets of the heart.

PSALM 44:20–21

I pray, God, that my husband will be
watchful, and strengthen the things
which remain, that are ready to die, for
Jesus has not found his works perfect
before You.

REVELATION 3:2

I pray that my husband will take heed to
himself, and diligently keep himself,
lest he forget the things his eyes have seen,
and lest they depart from his heart all
the days of his life.

DEUTERONOMY 4:9

I pray, God, that my husband returns to
You, and You will return to him.

MALACHI 3:7

I pray that my husband will look diligently
lest he fall short of Your grace, God;
and lest any root of bitterness spring up
causing trouble, and by this he becomes
defiled.

HEBREWS 12:15

I pray that after my husband has escaped
the pollutions of the world through the

knowledge of his Lord and Savior Jesus
Christ, that he not become again
entangled in them and overcome.

2 PETER 2:20

44

STRENGTH

God, I call upon You now to give my husband more strength than ever before. I pray Your word that You will increase his strength according to Your word, and I ask You to do that even as I pray Your word. In Jesus' precious name I pray. Amen.

God, in accordance with Your Word...

I pray, God, that You give power to my husband, who is weak, and that You increase his strength.

ISAIAH 40:29

I pray that my husband shall wait on You, LORD, and that he shall renew his strength. I pray that he shall mount up with wings like eagles, that he shall run and not be weary, and that he shall walk and not faint.

ISAIAH 40:31

◆

I pray that my husband will fear not, for You are with him. I pray that he will be not dismayed, for You are his God. I pray that You will strengthen him and help him and that You will uphold him with Your righteous right hand.

ISAIAH 41:10

◆

I pray that You, Lord, are my husband's rock and his fortress and his deliverer; his God, his strength, in whom he will trust; his shield and the horn of his salvation, his stronghold. I pray that he will call upon You, LORD, who is worthy to be praised; so shall he be saved from his enemies.

PSALM 18:2–3

I pray that You, LORD, are my husband's
light and his salvation. Whom shall he
fear?

PSALM 27:1

———————◆———————

I pray, God, that You will strengthen my
husband according to Your word.

PSALM 119:28

———————◆———————

I pray that my husband will be strengthened
with all might, according to Your
glorious power, God.

COLOSSIANS 1:11

———————◆———————

I pray that my husband can do all things
through Christ who strengthens him.

PHILIPPIANS 4:13

I pray that You, God, will grant my husband,
according to the riches of Your glory,
to be strengthened with might through
Your Spirit.

EPHESIANS 3:16

---◆---

I pray that my husband will be strong in
You, Lord, and in the power of Your
might. I pray that he will put on the whole
armor of God, that he may be able to
stand against the wiles of the devil. For he
does not wrestle against flesh and blood,
but against principalities, against powers,
against the rulers of the darkness of
this age, against spiritual hosts of
wickedness in the heavenly places.

EPHESIANS 6:10-12

---◆---

I pray that my husband will take up Your
whole armor, God, that he may be able
to withstand in the evil day, and having
done all, to stand. I pray that he will
stand therefore, having girded his waist

with truth, having put on the breastplate
of righteousness, and having shod his feet
with the preparation of the gospel of
peace; above all, taking the shield of faith
with which he will be able to quench
all the fiery darts of the wicked one. I pray
also that he will take the helmet of
salvation, and the sword of the Spirit,
which is the word of God, praying
always with all prayer and supplication in
the Spirit.

EPHESIANS 6:13–18

45

TEMPTED

Jesus, Your word says that You know how to deliver my husband out of temptations. I pray right now that You will now and forevermore deliver the husband that I love so much from any temptation that he may encounter. I pray Your word for him in this area, and I trust You to do as Your word promises. In Your name I pray. Amen.

God, in accordance
with Your Word...

I pray that You, Lord, know how to deliver
my husband out of temptations.

2 PETER 2:9

I pray that sin shall not have dominion
over my husband, for he is not under
law but under grace.

ROMANS 6:14

I pray, LORD, that Your word my husband
has hidden in his heart, that he might
not sin against You!

PSALM 119:11

I pray, Lord, that my husband will not say
when he is tempted, "I am tempted by
God"; for You cannot be tempted by evil,
nor do You Yourself tempt anyone. For
he is tempted when he is drawn away by
his own desires and enticed. Then, when
desire has conceived, it gives birth to sin;
and sin, when it is full-grown, brings
forth death. I pray that my husband will
not be deceived.

JAMES 1:13–15

I pray that if my husband confesses and
forsakes his sins he will have mercy.

PROVERBS 28:13

I pray that if my husband confesses his sins, You are faithful and just to forgive him his sins and to cleanse him from all unrighteousness.

1 JOHN 1:9

———————◆———————

I pray that no temptation has overtaken my husband except such as is common to man; but You, God, are faithful, and will not allow him to be tempted beyond what he is able, but with the temptation You will also make the way of escape, that he may be able to bear it.

1 CORINTHIANS 10:13

———————◆———————

I pray that my husband does not have a High Priest who cannot sympathize with his weaknesses, but was in all points tempted as he is, yet without sin. Let him therefore come boldly to the throne of grace, that he may obtain mercy and find grace to help in time of need.

HEBREWS 4:15–16

I pray, Jesus, that You are able to aid my
husband who is tempted.

HEBREWS 2:18

I pray that my husband will be sober and
vigilant; because his adversary the devil
walks about like a roaring lion, seeking
whom he may devour. I pray that he
will resist him, steadfast in the faith,
knowing that the same sufferings are
experienced by his Christian brothers in
the world.

1 PETER 5:8–9

I pray that my husband will be strong in
You, Lord, and in the power of Your
might. I pray that he will put on Your
whole armor, God, that he may be able
to stand against the wiles of the devil, and
that above all, he takes the shield of
faith with which he will be able to quench
all the fiery darts of the wicked one.

EPHESIANS 6:10–11, 16

I pray, God, that my husband will resist the devil and that he will flee from him.

JAMES 4:7

———— ◆ ————

I pray, God, that He who is in my husband is greater than he who is in the world.

1 JOHN 4:4

———— ◆ ————

I pray, Lord, that my husband will count it all joy when he falls into various trials, knowing that the testing of his faith produces patience. I pray that blessed is my husband who endures temptation; for when he has been approved, he will receive the crown of life which You have promised to those who love You.

JAMES 1:2–3, 12

———— ◆ ————

I pray that You, God, are able to keep my husband from stumbling and to present

him faultless before the presence of Your
glory with exceeding joy.

JUDE 1:24

———————— ◆ ————————

I pray that in this my husband will greatly
rejoice, though now for a little while, if
need be, he has been grieved by various
trials, that the genuineness of his faith,
being much more precious than gold that
perishes, though it is tested by fire,
may be found to praise, honor, and glory
at the revelation of Jesus Christ.

1 PETER 1:6–7

46

TROUBLES

Lord, Your word says that You will allow no more troubles than my husband can bear. Today, even now, I pray Your word to overcome any troubles my husband may have. Please honor Your words in my prayers and take care of and strengthen him. It is in the authority of the name of Jesus that I pray. Amen.

God, in accordance
with Your Word...

I pray that my husband shall obtain joy
and gladness and that sorrow and
sighing shall flee away.

ISAIAH 51:11

I pray that my husband will be anxious for
nothing, but in everything by prayer
and supplication, with thanksgiving, will

let his requests be made known to You,
God, and Your peace, which surpasses all
understanding, will guard his heart and
mind through Christ Jesus.

PHILIPPIANS 4:6–7

I pray, God, that You will comfort my
husband in all his tribulation, that he
may be able to comfort those who are in
any trouble, with the comfort with
which he himself is comforted by You.

2 CORINTHIANS 1:4

I pray, God, that my husband does not
worry about tomorrow, for tomorrow
will worry about its own things.

MATTHEW 6:34

I pray that all things work together for good
to my husband who loves You, God, to

he who is called according to Your
purpose.

ROMANS 8:28

———— ◆ ————

I pray that my husband will be glad and
rejoice in Your mercy, God, for You
have considered his trouble. You have
known his soul in adversities, and have
not shut him up into the hand of the
enemy; You have set his feet in a wide
place.

PSALM 31:7–8

———— ◆ ————

I pray that my husband's help comes from
You, LORD, who made heaven and earth.

PSALM 121:2

———— ◆ ————

I pray that my husband will come boldly
to the throne of grace, that he may

obtain mercy and find grace to help him
in time of need.

HEBREWS 4:16

---◆---

I pray, God, that my husband will cast all
his care upon You, for You care for him.

1 PETER 5:7

---◆---

I pray, O God, that my husband always
remembers that You are good, a
stronghold in his day of trouble; and that
You know that he trusts in You.

NAHUM 1:7

---◆---

I pray that though my husband is hard
pressed on every side, he is not crushed;
he is perplexed, but not in despair;
persecuted, but not forsaken; struck
down, but not destroyed.

2 CORINTHIANS 4:8–9

I pray that though my husband walks in
the midst of trouble, You, God, will
revive him. You will stretch out Your hand
against the wrath of his enemies, and
Your right hand will save him.

PSALM 138:7

I pray that my husband will not let his heart
be troubled. I pray that he believes in
You, God, and also in Jesus.

JOHN 14:1

I pray, God, that when my husband passes
through the waters, You will be with
him. And through the rivers, they shall not
overflow him. When he walks through
the fire, he shall not be burned, nor shall
the flame scorch him.

ISAIAH 43:2

47

WAITING ON GOD

Heavenly Father, I really do believe that the most important thing that I can do is to pray Your very words and thoughts over my husband. My prayers today will be Your words from Your word. Hear my prayers, and help my husband to wait on You. I pray everything in Jesus' wonderful name. Amen.

God, in accordance with Your Word...

I pray, God, that my husband will say in that day: "Behold, this is my God. I have waited for Him, and He will save me. This is the LORD; I have waited for Him. I will be glad and rejoice in His salvation."

ISAIAH 25:9

———————— ◆ ————————

I pray that my husband has become a partaker of Christ if he holds the

beginning of his confidence steadfast to
the end.

HEBREWS 3:14

———————◆———————

I pray that my husband waits for You, LORD,
that his soul waits, and in Your word
he does hope.

PSALM 130:5

———————◆———————

I pray that my husband will wait on You,
LORD, and that he will be of good
courage. I pray also that You will strengthen
his heart.

PSALM 27:14

———————◆———————

I pray, God, that my husband's soul waits
silently for You alone and that his
expectation is from You.

PSALM 62:5

I pray, O God, that my husband will hold fast the confession of his hope without wavering, for You who promised are faithful.

HEBREWS 10:23

———◆———

I pray that my husband shall wait on You, LORD, and that he shall renew his strength. I pray also that he shall mount up with wings like eagles and that he shall run and not be weary and walk and not faint.

ISAIAH 40:31

———◆———

I pray that my husband's soul waits for You, LORD, that You are his help and his shield.

PSALM 33:20

48

WORRIED

Most Precious God, I pray Your very words over the worries of my husband. You have promised to not let his heart be troubled if he will cast his cares on You. Based on Your words I pray that all worry will flee from him and that his joy will return to him. All of my prayers I pray in Jesus' name. Amen.

God, in accordance with Your Word...

I pray, God, that my husband will not let his heart be troubled.

JOHN 14:1

I pray that my husband will cast all his cares upon You, God, for You care for him.

1 PETER 5:7

I pray that my husband will lie down in peace, and sleep; for You alone, O LORD, make him dwell in safety.

PSALM 4:8

I pray that You, God, will keep my husband in perfect peace, he whose mind is stayed on You, because he trusts in You.

ISAIAH 26:3

I pray, God, that my husband will let Your peace rule in his heart.

COLOSSIANS 3:15

I pray that my husband will be anxious for nothing, but in everything by prayer and supplication, with thanksgiving, will let his requests be made known to You, God; and Your peace, which surpasses all

understanding, will guard his heart and
mind through Christ Jesus.

PHILIPPIANS 4:6–7

I pray, God, that You shall supply all my
husband's needs according to Your
riches in glory by Christ Jesus.

PHILIPPIANS 4:19

I pray that my husband will not worry
about his life, what he will eat or what
he will drink; nor about his body, what he
will put on. I pray that he will seek first
Your kingdom, God, and Your
righteousness, and all these things shall
be added to him.

MATTHEW 6:25, 33

I pray, LORD, that when my husband lies
down, he will not be afraid. I pray that

he will lie down and his sleep will be
sweet.

PROVERBS 3:24

---◆---

I pray that my husband will say of You,
LORD, "He is my refuge and my fortress;
my God, in Him I will trust."

PSALM 91:2

---◆---

I pray, O God, that great peace has my
husband who loves Your law, and
nothing causes him to stumble.

PSALM 119:165

---◆---

I pray, Jesus, that Your peace You leave
with my husband and that Your peace
You give to him; not as the world gives do
You give to him. Let not his heart be
troubled, neither let it be afraid.

JOHN 14:27

Seminars conducted by Lee Roberts include *Praying God's Will*, *Avoiding Failure in Your Christian Walk*, and *The Businessman, the Salesman, and God!*

More information on these seminars can be obtained by writing Lee Roberts, P.O. Box 671465, Marietta, GA 30067-0025, or by calling 404-956-8550.